The Queen of Hearts

The Life of Zelma Louise Roth Studebaker
Second Edition

Gary W. Studebaker and Amy L. Powell

WIPF & STOCK · Eugene, Oregon

Wipf and Stock Publishers
199 W 8th Ave, Suite 3
Eugene, OR 97401

The Queen of Hearts
The Life of Zelma Louise Roth Studebaker, Second Edition
By Studebaker, Gary W. and Powell, Amy
Copyright©1997 by Studebaker, Gary W.
ISBN 13: 978-1-5326-4634-8
Publication date 3/19/2018
Previously published by KNI, Incorporated, 1997

Contents

Preface

Zelma Studebaker was a common woman who had many uncommon and prized characteristics that continue to be remembered long after her life of 87 years. Her story and relationships with family and friends remain prominent, simply because she devoted time to a life that valued respect and acceptance of people. Even individuals who were generations removed from her age group felt they were included and supported. Such relationships were her strength, an area where she thrived.

Her life is portrayed herein in her stories, poetry, humor, humanitarian values, Christian beliefs and narratives from Zelma's friends and relatives. Her life is also a story of persistence and her belief in being productive with God given abilities. She believed in equal rights and volunteer service to people in need. Therefore she participated in service projects and was proud to see her entire family engage in volunteer service to address human needs.

As a writer, she saved her many poems, stories and compositions in notebooks and diaries over a span of many years. She probably never suspected that her poetry and stories would ever be read by many people, but Zelma's son Gary, the family historian, had been saving her poems and stories for publication so she asked him to take her writings. Gary and Amy Powell, Zelma's granddaughter teamed up for this biography project. Amy collected written memoirs from the grandchildren. She also gathered information from her personal talks and recorded interviews with Zelma and other relatives. Gary and Amy wrote the original biography of Zelma's life published in 1997. With the emergence of more information: photos, family publications, family reunions and the development of online bookstores, the second edition of her biography has resulted in this publication.

It must be stated that the impact and implications of family roots are far-reaching. Having experienced the outcomes of our own published family biographies, we have found them to have a major influence on the way we think about our own lives as well as our ancestors. Our grasp of their triumphs, hardships and previously unknown facts make a difference in our lives as stated in the following observation:

> "When you study history, you're really studying yourself. Every bit of history I've uncovered about my own family has some remnant in myself." - John Sedgwick

It is for these reasons that the children of Zelma and Stanley Studebaker credit their parents for influencing their children's participation in ongoing family reunions at various locations throughout the country, the production of biographies and autobiographies, and other events that spark the fascination and appreciation of family roots. Some of the grandchildren of Zelma and Stanley have expressed their plans to continue some of these same traditions.

Acknowledgements

Much advice and reviewing of this script were necessary for the publication of the life of Zelma Studebaker. Many individuals wrote descriptions of their relationship with Zelma. From Mary Ann Cornell we received boxes of Zelma's poetry, short stories, autobiography, documents, audio recordings and artifacts as well as photos. A review and advice from Ron Studebaker was significant in the production of this project.

All the children of Zelma and Stanley contributed photos and written descriptions to help tell Zelma's story. We wish to acknowledge the contributions of the following individuals: Stanley Studebaker, Zelma Studebaker, Pauline Dennis, Mary Ann Cornell, Milton Mishler, Julia Lutz, Craig Huffaker, Cindy Huffaker, Jill Morris, Brad Huffaker, Brian Huffaker, Lowell Studebaker, Diane Gillespie, Dan Studebaker, Dave Studebaker, Nancy Smith, Alison Bucchi, Phil Smith, Linda Post, Jim Biller, Jenny Sprecher, Jim S. Biller, Ron Studebaker, Evonne Studebaker, Ranya Studebaker, Tarik Studebaker, Kendra Sherman, Chad Studebaker, Susan Studebaker, Ramona Studebaker, Doug Studebaker, Linda Buhl Studebaker and Mackenzie Studebaker.

Our thanks to the contributors,

Gary Studebaker and Amy Powell

Chapter 1

The Early Years

"We inherit from our ancestors gifts so often taken for granted…We are links between the ages, containing past and present expectations, sacred memories and future promise."

Edward Sellner

It was April 19, 1907 when Zelma Louise Roth was born in Englewood, Ohio, a town of less than 100 people at the time. Theodore Roosevelt was the president. Horse drawn wagons and buggies were the means of transportation. Automobiles were beginning to make an appearance on the gravel roads of Englewood. Kerosene lanterns were used to provide lighting to homes. It would be few years later when electric lights would be introduced in the streets and homes in Englewood, Ohio. Since Zelma's father was an electrician, he was one of the pioneers who first introduced electricity in Englewood and nearby towns.

Zelma was the second child born to Fred and Elnora Roth. Zelma's life of 87 years would leave some extraordinary memories of the things she did, said and wrote. She vividly recalls her childhood memories and a life that was filled with curiosity and a desire to be a part of it all. She learned the characteristics of honesty, endurance and hard work from her parents and relatives in her environment. Her early development and thoughts were influenced by her family life which included story telling adventures by her Grandpa Coelestine. She was exposed to nursery rhymes, Aesop's Fables, classical literature, poetry and the Bible. She also saw uncles who were inventive, enterprising and productive. She remembered these same relatives as the ones who brought fun and humor to family gatherings. It would be these same interesting people, places and stories that would deeply influence her future life. Her values and personality would be strongly shaped by an array of early encounters which ranged from solid family nurturing to tragedy and hardship along the way. The following is Zelma's autobiography of her early years.

> The big cuckoo clock on the wall ticked away as I stood quietly by the big front window waiting for Grandpa to wake up from his brief afternoon nap. Outside an occasional horse and buggy passed on the dusty Old National Road or a neighbor walking to the grocery or Post Office on the gravel path just beyond our picket fence. Life in Englewood in 1910 seemed to my barely three-year old perception a very satisfactory world of smooth-running just-rightness.
>
> Grandpa stirred in his big comfortable rocking chair beside me. I hurried to make sure he would not doze off again. Grandpa, tell me another story," I said hugging his knees. Today, 80 years later, I can still see the twinkle in his blue eyes, his hand smoothing the long reddish-brown beard as he recognized my

presence and the familiar demand. "Well, we'd better have an apple I guess," he chuckled reaching for his pocket-knife. "And don't forget the old newspaper."

Running to the kitchen I was back in a wink with the biggest red apple in the bowl and a section of paper which I spread on the floor between Grandpa's feet. Sitting on the pretty green rose-bedecked carpet squarely in front of him, I watched the familiar routine between us. Grandpa opened his knife and inserted it at the stem end of the apple. Slowly and carefully he began to peel and turn it so that a gradually lengthening red spiral began to dangle between the apple and the newspaper. At the same time he began the story. What a wondrous magical treat for my eyes and ears! I might hear a tale about my Grandpa's boyhood in Germany or his voyage to America in a sailing ship as an eighteen year old or he might tell me about the many wild and fascinating animals in the African jungles of which he seemed to have an endless amount of knowledge. I sat spellbound, totally carried away yet knowing when the knife made the last carving trip around the blossom end and that spiral fell on the paper, the story would end. But there would still be the warm satisfaction and delight to savor in the completion of our little ritual. Grandpa cut the apple in half and removed the core. Together we ate and the bond between the seventy-eight year old and the three year old grew strong.

This episode from my childhood is one of the earliest and most treasured memories. It was repeated often and I'm sure the dangling peel sometimes broke off or the story did not always end especially at the moment the spiral dropped, but in my memory those variations did not exist.

My grandfather, Coelestine Leiber was born in 1832 near the village of Niedereschach in Southern Germany. He was one of the youngest of ten children in the family. Because of the severe economic hardships and oppression brought on by the war, it was extremely difficult for the family to make a living from their small plots of ground. In order to ease the struggle for survival, the three younger brothers and a sister decided to go to America. There they felt they would have an opportunity to find useful work and establish themselves in the fields of their training and experience. Thus they would ease the burden at home and be able to send some supplies and other aid to their parents.

They made preparations in late July of 1850 when Coelestine was 18 years old. He and his brothers John, Anthony, Otto and their sister, Theresa left with a few belongings in a horse-drawn cart for Rotterdam. Here they embarked on a sailing ship bound for New York. Shortly after departure the wind changed with increasing force. Eventually the ship could not be controlled and they were blown back to port. Finally they began their voyage again and enjoyed many days of fine weather and smooth sailing as well as good companionship with their fellow travelers. But once again the ship was rocked and tossed so violently by a storm that the passengers became frightened and desperately sick.

Grandpa said they were thrown about by waives that "appeared to be 40 feet high" and people prayed to God for help. When the storm abated many were too sick to eat for days. But in early October they docked in New York Harbor.

The little group found a place to stay at a nearby lodging house for a few weeks where they could get rest and their bearings before moving on. John was thinking of finding a place in good farming and dairy country, maybe Wisconsin. Anthony favored a home and work in Chicago and he settled in that area. Coelestine was eager to find a home in an agriculture area, perhaps a small rural village where he could establish himself in the business of veterinary medicine for which he had trained. He began to make inquiries of fellow boarders and lay his plans as he prepared to head westward.

Life in the boarding house must have been lively and interesting indeed as working people and newly arriving immigrants met and mingled, especially at meal time. Encounters in such a fertile environment often set the course of one's life in unforeseen directions as Grandpa's experience attests. He told us his story many times with a sly smile.

A fellow boarder tried to persuade Grandpa that he should marry before setting out on such a venture but Grandpa insisted that he had no time nor interest in finding a wife at that point. The man reasoned that with a good wife to accompany, encourage and support him and to cook meals, it could be much easier. Of course, he had someone in mind. Among the crew of domestic workers in the kitchen he said, was a sturdy young German girl, very strong and of good character as well as ruddy-cheeked and nice looking. He proposed that when supper was served that evening and the girls began to bring food to the tables, he would wink at Grandpa when "the right one appeared" and he should "keep an eye on her" as she worked. If he liked her and was interested, he was to wink back and the man would arrange an introduction. Grandpa looked and winked. Two weeks later he and Elnora Sunkle were married. He never filled us in on what transpired in those two weeks to persuade Elnora to say "I do" on such a short notice but his grandchildren found it amusing that he always cautioned them not to be that hasty in marrying because "It might not always work out so well." However, theirs was a good marriage lasting more than 40 years when Grandma died. They had 11 children of which my mother was youngest. Together the couple came to Ohio and were attracted to the beauty of the Stillwater Valley. They settled in the little village of Englewood on the Stillwater River 10 miles north of Dayton.

Their house was on the Old National Road which was the main east-west thoroughfare in town. One short block east, the Dayton-Covington Pike intersected the road just before it sloped down to the old covered bridge across the river. The house was of log construction with wood siding and the inside walls were plastered lath. A large roomy kitchen served also as dining room and sitting room with a door opening onto the porch. Two doors on the adjacent wall led into a parlor and a bedroom. Upstairs there were three bedrooms and a porch directly over the lower porch. Leading off one end of the lower porch was another building which was called the "summer kitchen." It was used for that purpose as well as for the laundry room. It also had a porch with two pumps which furnished good cold well water and rain water. A barn at the back of the lot had horse stalls, a pen for a cow and a hay loft. Nearby was a chicken house and a small hog house. Grandpa added a 10 foot grape arbor which arched over the walk and led from the porch to the front gate. There children were born here, grew up and married. This was Grandpa's home for the rest of his life and it became the home of my parents and all their children until Grandpa died in 1916 at age 86. Later it was sold to settle his estate. I was 9 years old at that time so all of my early childhood memories are centered in and around this house and community. For that reason I have described it in some detail.

Soon after coming to Englewood, Grandpa was kept busy with calls to treat livestock for the farmers in the surrounding area and he soon became known as a reliable and trustworthy veterinarian. He had a love for animals and was well versed in the use of plants, seeds, herbs, roots and bark for medicinal purposes. With these ingredients, many of which he gathered locally and some he purchased by mail order, he developed, processed and sold a powdered product which he packaged under the label "Dr. Liber's Horse Powder – Good for Man or Beast." I can remember more than once being given a spoonful of this pungent yellowish powder dissolved in water to relieve a stomach ache and wondering why since I was neither man nor beast.

Grandpa had been born into a devout Catholic family and had served as an altar boy in his youth in Germany. Before coming to America as his parents were bidding their children goodbye, their father admonished them to hold fast to their faith in God and to align themselves with a church as soon as they had settled. He said it was most important to join a group of believers; whether or not they chose the Catholic or a Protestant church. It was interesting that Grandpa and Grandma became members of the old German Baptist Church sometimes called Old Order Dunkard. They wore the plain garb, lived very simple and tried to follow the scriptural teachings "for the glory of God and their neighbor's good." Their children learned early to respect God and all his creation and to respect each other and all persons regardless of race, religion or social status. Fairness, compassion, honesty and hard work were built into their characters, more by example than by hard and fast house rules. A healthy sense of humor permeated the make-up of each one and in fact, seemed to trickle through the veins of their descendants, which contributes to the fact that family gatherings are happy and relaxing occasions, pleasant to anticipate and look back on.

Three of their children died in infancy. Fred married Mary Penrod and lived in Lewisburg, Ohio. Mary (Molly) married Joe Toprano and moved to Farmersville, Ohio and Caroline (Collie) was married to John Sink, a railroad inspector in Winchester, Indiana. Charles, Ed, Gus, Les and Nora, my mother, spent their entire lives in Englewood, all within two blocks of each other. As his sons grew to manhood, a two story building was built beside the house on the corner of what is now National Road and Walnut Street.

As their business card proclaimed, this was the shop of C. Leiber and Sons, Wagon makers. Grandpa with Uncle Ed, Uncle Gus and Uncle Les began a thriving business of making their version of a serviceable covered utility wagon for farmers. With a seat across the front and ample space behind, they could transport passengers, goods and small equipment, all framed and covered by a cloth-coated covering resembling leather. They were designed in a style which was a sort of forerunner to our modern covered pickup trucks except of course they were literally one-horse powered vehicles, fueled by oats and corn with a top speed dependent on one's ability to accelerate the horse. At the side of the shop a wide ramp led up to the second floor and the wagons were drawn up to be painted in a fairly dust free room.

When Uncle Ed and Uncle Gus married they set up their own blacksmith shop just north of the downtown intersection of National Road and Covington Pike. Uncle Les continued making wagons and added lawn mower and saw sharpening when Grandpa retired. Soon automobiles began to outnumber wagons and his shop modernized into a busy Texaco service station which he operated with Aunt Elizabeth's help until he retired.

At the time of Grandma Leiber's death, my mother, Nora took over all household duties and the care of Grandpa and Uncle Les who was not yet married. She had learned well the arts of cooking, baking, sewing and managing a home. Monday was always washday and Tuesday was ironing day. She did mending on Wednesday, general cleaning on Friday and baking the weekend's supply of bread and coffee cakes. Saturday was a day to make several pies and usually a cake or cookies. Plenty of noodles were made too. Such things as sewing, canning and reworking old clothing into braided rugs or piecing comforters and quilts were done in between, but she followed this general work plan most of her life. Growing flowers was one of her great loves and the gorgeous riot of colors she created every summer attested to her green thumb.

Soon after the turn of the century, D.C and P (Dayton, Covington and Piqua) traction line was built from Dayton to Covington and eventually to Piqua. One of the young electrical workers, Fred Roth, found room and board at Ed and Anna Leiber's home. Thus, he and Nora met and as time passed were mutually attracted to each other. On Christmas day in 1902 at "high noon" according to the wedding invitation, they were married at the home of the bride. My father was 25 and my mother was 28. She made her wedding dress of beautiful soft navy taffeta. When I was three years old, she made a pretty spring coat for me from this dress with heavy cream colored lace overlying the collar, a front panel and "silver" filigree buttons.

My father was born to Jacob and Louise Swope Roth. The family lived in High Hill, Ohio, a small community near Zanesville. My Grandfather Roth had been a cattle driver, moving cattle from the Hamilton, Ohio area to Greenville and areas north. He met and married Grandma near Hamilton when she was about 14 and extremely shy, she said. In fact, she was so timid that when Grandpa decided to take her on a brief honeymoon to Cincinnati she asked her girl friend to go along, which she did, having an adjoining room.

Their small farm at High Hill was not too productive and Grandpa's daily grind of trying to make a living apparently brought out the worst in his ill-tempered and damaging nature. He hired his sons out to work when they were 10 to 15 years old for whatever pay they could get. My father told of working for a farmer milking many cows and cleaning the barn all winter Monday to Saturday night for 25 cents per week, which he had to turn over to his father. He told of his brothers going barefoot during weekdays, winter and summer because they were allowed to wear their one pair of shoes for going to church only. Grandma Roth was of a quiet kindly nature, a loving mother and a hard worker, but unable to persuade Grandpa to be less harsh. Eventually the sons, as they became 18, left to find good jobs and all except Jacob and John came to Dayton where Charlie had established the Fulton Fish Market on East Fourth Street. Ed and Bill also had their own seafood markets.

My parents moved to a house on Vincent Street in Dayton right after their marriage as my father had a job with Dayton Power and Light. Uncle Charlie's brother-in-law, Ora Hutchins, was an executive at DP&L and hired and trained him to be an able and efficient electrician. Very shortly after they moved word came that Grandpa Roth had met with an accident and died. While working in his hog pen, a large boar had become irritated and bit him in the groin. We never heard my father or Grandma speak with bitterness or anger of Grandpa's hardness or severe demands. They simply stated the sad facts when it was mentioned at all. In fact my father said the experience set his strong determination to appreciate his family and show them that he cared about them, and he did that indeed.

My parents named their first child Orville Edison. At that time Grandpa Leiber and Uncle Les had hired a housekeeper. Evidently they made a poor choice because she couldn't cook. Meals were scanty, underdone or burned and she seemed not interested in learning. After a couple of years both men lost weight and became very sick so my mother went to take care of them. It was during this time that my baby brother, Orville Edison, died. He was six weeks of age when he contracted pneumonia and died in only a few days. Grandpa then offered my parents his home for the remainder of his life in exchange for his care. They moved back to Englewood and this proved to be a happy solution for all concerned.

On April 19, 1907 the robust voice of a wailing infant was heard disturbing the early morning peace in Englewood, thus I made my debut I'm told. At the time my mother's nephew, Charlie Sink had a lady friend, Zelma Wheelock and my parents liked her name. So I was named for her and my paternal grandmother.

I was three years old when Emerson, my first brother was born. I remember the white-aproned housekeeper who came for two weeks. As I sat by the cook stove and watched her give him a bath, she asked whether I liked my baby brother. I said, "I don't like the kind that cries and wets like that." But soon I adjusted to him and never felt at all jealous or left out. Rather I felt quite important as a big sister and caretaker and he kept me on my toes because he was determined to put things in his mouth. I dug everything from buttons and stones to lightening bugs out of his mouth.

A most frightening experience was my heroic effort to rescue him from a big bear. I was barely four and he was just toddling unsteadily. My mother was baking bread and she told me to take him out under the maple tree to see the horses and wagons go by and watch him carefully. Everything went well as he played just outside our gate in the grass. We watched as the train crossed the National Road just beyond the grain elevator west of our house. Suddenly I saw a man with a bear, probably passengers who had just got off the train coming down the road toward us. I was panic stricken and tried to lead Emerson to the safety of the house but he was totally obsessed with watching the bear and had no intention of coming with me. In desperation I flung my arms around his kicking, squirming body and lugged him screaming into the kitchen, dumped him in the chimney corner and sat on him too exhausted to talk. Finally I was able to explain to my mother that a big bear was about to get him. She thought it was my wild imagination but because of my near hysteria she took me to the window to check. And there went the bear lumbering along behind a man who was leading him by a chain around his neck. There was a wire muzzle over his mouth and the man carried a black box with a long wooden leg underneath - the proverbial old organ grinder with his trained bear. My mother explained that they sometimes visit small towns and give a street performance. People gathered to watch and listen as the bear danced or waddled from side to side while the owner cranked out his lively tunes. People threw small change into his tin cup which he passed around.

Grandpa took me to the show that evening but I never let go of his hand. My mother never doubted my trustworthiness as a baby-watcher after that. Among other little cameo scenes that flash sharply into memory from my very early childhood is our old Edison phonograph, a box-like cabinet which sat on a small chest. The loud speaker was a large horn and there was a crank which activated the mechanism to play the cylinder records. As an electrician, my father had a great admiration for Thomas Edison and his inventions. He liked to play the records and tell me about Edison. I remember listening to Caruso's tenor voice singing in Italian while I looked at the picture of the little black and white dog that also appeared to be listening intently. Under the picture were the words "His Master's Voice."

In that year I also remember Uncle Les took a trip and brought me a beautiful big picture story book with a shiny hard cover on which was a picture of a little boy in a blue sailor suit launching a toy boat. Inside the cover Uncle Les inscribed, "To Zelma from Uncle Les – 1910" which for some reason made me feel very important. It was a highly prized treasure for years.

Books became a favorite pastime long before I could read, and the words made wonderful pictures in my mind as Grandpa and my parents read the stories and poems over and over to me. I learned dozens of nursery rhymes and loved to pretend I was reading them as I represented each one by looking at the pictures.

While I was being taught to be truthful, obedient, and honest, to love God and all people, it was all reinforced by Bible stories and Aesop's Fables. Etched in my mind today are the deep impressions made by listening to: "The Fox and the Grapes," "The Ant and the Grasshopper," "Daniel in the Lion's Den." "Moses in the Bulrushes," "Feeding the Five Thousand" and other stories. My Bible Story Picture Book inspired the dramatic urge in me. An old quilt thrown over the backs of several kitchen chairs became Noah's Ark, the lion's den or the walls of Jericho which came tumbling down amid deafening shouts after the Israelites (my dolls and I) marched around it blowing imaginary trumpets for seven days.

My cousins, Glenna, Helen and Esther just up the street, had a piano and I wanted to learn to play it but my parents said I must first go to school and become a good reader. In the meantime, not to become discouraged, I made a fairly satisfactory piano and stool under the lilac bush by the cave. I upturned a galvanized wash tub and an old milk crock and decided to practice earnestly until such a time that I could go to school and learn the necessary skills to take piano lessons. I drummed my fingers on that tub and sang nursery rhymes, hymns and whatever compositions my mind dictated. I recall rendering quite an impressive dirge on the occasion of a funeral which Ruth Berger, a neighbor girl and I arranged for one of Grandpa's recently hatched baby chicks. We had chased it around the barn too fast and too far. She preached briefly but solemnly while I provided soft doleful music. We buried the fuzzy little yellow body under the quince tree.

Fred and Elnora (Nora) Roth, Zelma's parents were very caring and hard-working people. Nora was a tall gracious and soft spoken woman and she was very resourceful at the many household responsibilities. She made clothing for the family on her foot treadle sewing machine and was skillful at making colorful rugs and rag dolls for her children and grandchildren. She is especially remembered for making her own butter and noodles as well as delicious coffee cakes and breads. She even made her own soap. The family didn't have to buy very much since they had their own truck patch which provided many vegetables. They also had a supply of eggs and milk as they raised their own chickens and had a cow.

Zelma's father, Fred had a sense of humor and enjoyed playing games with his children and grandchildren. His grandchildren remember how he would tickle them and he especially liked to play Chinese Checkers with them after which he would give them a chunk of chocolate. On some occasions he would throw pennies in the air for them to find. Fred came from a very poor family where sometimes food and clothing were scarce.

As an electrician Fred did most of his early electrical wiring when the street lights were installed in Englewood in 1911. The disastrous flood of 1913 led to the construction of the Englewood Dam. Fred worked as an electrician on that project from 1918 to 1922.

Zelma's parents belonged to the Mennonite Church where it was Fred's job to ring the church bells on Sunday mornings. He was a small statured man, so small that the ropes pulled him off the ground on their upward swing. Bible reading was a regular habit in their house with Fred doing the reading and praying each evening. The children learned at an early age to be helpful to less fortunate people. Since their home was on the National Road, many travelers passed by and sometime homeless people knocked on their door asking for food. Zelma described how her mother prepared her to be concerned for these people by allowing her to take food to them. Her mother explained that even the handicapped, have a right to have a job and to be treated with fairness like everyone else.

Her father liked to chew tobacco. The smell of tobacco permeated his electrical supply shop. The door of his nice black car was always stained with tobacco juice from his spitting habit. His tobacco chewing custom was so intense that on one occasion when he was in the hospital and near death, he told Zelma that if he had another chew of tobacco, he'd be alright. Zelma didn't have the heart to deny his request so she went right out and bought a pack of Mail Pouch Tobacco for him.

Zelma's siblings were: Orville Edison, first born who died of Pneumonia a few months after birth in 1906. Zelma was the second child and there were three children born after her, Emerson, Pauline and Loyal. The family often enjoyed visits with nearby relatives. Her mother was good about writing distant relatives to keep in touch and her writing was artistic and legible. She always taught her children to be well dressed and clean. Zelma was always proud of her hair ribbons which her mother bought to match her dresses.

Among the many activities Zelma enjoyed during her childhood years was playing in the sandbox, swinging, lying in the yard watching the stars with her brothers and sister and playing with her dolls in the shed which she used as a playhouse. It was during her early years that she learned to play Checkers, Parcheesi, Andy Over, hop scotch and jump rope. The family also had a dog named Puff that she helped care for.

It was a treat for Zelma to go with her dad in the horse drawn cart to help him sell fish in the rural areas surrounding Englewood. This was Fred's second job. She also collected Indian artifacts that were so often found during and after the land excavation operations to build the Englewood Dam. Her collection included arrowheads as well as some flint stone axes.

When Zelma was 12 years old, her parents bought a piano for her. She took lessons and spent much time practicing. Playing the piano became an endearing hobby for the remainder of her life. Her dad and her brother, Emerson always had a harmonica which they both played. Her Grandfather Coelestine played the accordion, an instrument he brought with him from Germany. The family also had a Victrola which added to her music appreciation.
Zelma describes herself as curious and always interested in what was happening in her environment. When asked to describe a warm cozy place in her childhood, she said it was being with her grandfather, Coelestine. Zelma enjoyed going out into the wooded areas where she helped her grandfather collect various plants and tree bark which he used to make his veterinarian medicines.

She fondly remembered how quiet it was at the end of each story he read to her while they both thought about the importance of the story and what she had just learned. One of the stories that she vividly recalled was the devastation of war. He told her that all three of his sister's sons were killed in Germany in World War I. He explained to her that during the war, the Americans and Germans were fighting one another and sometimes relatives were on opposing sides. She never forgot how terrible that was.

During her elementary and junior high years, she walked to the nearby four room brick school house where one teacher taught the first four grades and another teacher taught the next four grades. Zelma was a smart student and always got her school work done ahead of time. Then she would listen to the older students being taught geography. Upon arriving at home, she would get the geography book out and learn for herself what the teacher had been teaching the older students. On one occasion when she was in the second grade, she was asked by the teacher of the upper grades to come to the front of the class to show his students how to work addition problems on the chalkboard. She was nervous about being "put on the spot" but thankful that she had successfully worked the problems for her older peers. At the conclusion of her demonstration, she quietly listened to the teacher reprimand his students by telling them, "It took a second grade student to show you older students how to do these addition problems! Now aren't you ashamed of yourselves?" After receiving a commendation for her excellent work in front of the older students, she was sent back to her seat feeling quietly proud of what she had just done.

One of her favorite activities was reading the comics in the newspaper. During her high school years, she took pleasure in reading stories and writing poetry. She developed a strong interest in poetry and literature in her school years where she learned to recite such favorites as The Village Blacksmith, The Friendly Cow, The Gingham Dog and the Calico Cat and the Cheerful Cherub. Many years later, she recited these same stories to her own children and grandchildren.

After Zelma had lived two years in the home where she was born, her parents moved to another nearby home on the hill on the south side of National Road in Englewood. She lived there until she was married. This home was remembered by Zelma's children as fun to visit because they had so many things to see and do. Behind the house as the hill sloped downward, was a large grape arbor where white and red grapes clustered for eating and making jellies and jams. There was also a chicken house where they helped gather eggs and some bee hives where the family collected their own honey. Fred's electrical shop was fun to explore because he had fascinating electrical fixtures, colorful tiffany lamp shades and the unforgettable smell of tobacco which he kept there.

At an early age Zelma knew she wanted to pursue a college education. She went on to become a teacher. She had learned the importance of saving at least some of her earnings. She saved her money in a tin can and her cousin, Charley Sink who worked in a bank, helped her start a savings account in the bank where he worked. During her high school years she earned money by working as a waitress in a hotel in Englewood. Another job was working at a factory where she cleaned and prepared sweetcorn to be sold.

In 1925 Zelma graduated from Randolph High School in Englewood with 25 members in her senior class. She was one of three of her classmates who went to college. In preparation for becoming a teacher, she attended Manchester College at North Manchester, Indiana for one year. Then she attended Wittenberg University in Springfield, Ohio for two semesters where she took classes during the summer. After completing six terms of college education, she began teaching grades one through four north of Dayton at the age of 18. This was during an era when women were allowed to teach after one year of college. During this period of time teaching was only available for men and unmarried women. It was the role of married women to stay at home and take care of the children. Such a rule was strictly enforced. Her salary was $100.00 per month which she considered good pay at the time. With her earnings she was able to buy her first car, an impressive maroon Model T Ford Coup.

Zelma became acquainted with Stanley Studebaker when they both attended Randolph High School where he was one class ahead of her. Pauline recalls Zelma's first date with Stanley. One summer day when Pauline, Zelma and their mother were sitting on the front porch, a car went by slowly as the young man waved. Zelma told them, "That was Stanley Studebaker and Lois told me the other day that he had his eye on me." Minutes later the telephone rang and Zelma answered. After the talk, she reported that it was Stanley Studebaker and that he had asked her for a date on Saturday night. Her mother said, "You're going out, aren't you? Pauline recalled that "Zelma was so shy that it caused her to fib!" She told him she couldn't go because she had already made plans. Her mother reminded her that she should have accepted the invitation. Zelma seemed to pay no attention but Stanley was persistent and got that first date the following Saturday. He picked her up in his Ford Coup and took her to the nearby town of Shiloh for an ice cream soda. His car had a shelf behind the seats where he had a radio which he was tinkering with to try to bring a station in more clearly.

According to Stanley they dated about six months going to church, the park, movies in Dayton and just talking at her house. Zelma was engaged at the age of 21 when Stanley gave her a diamond ring. On June 14, 1929 they were married at the Englewood Mennonite Church. Pauline sang, "I Love You Truly" and Milton Owen, Stanley's cousin sang, "Believe Me If All Those Enduring Young Charms." They went to Niagara Falls for their honeymoon in Zelma's Model T Ford. Stanley recalls the only mishap on the trip was when he decided to pick up a stray dog that he found along the road that had followed them for a few miles. Stanley thought it would be a good dog to herd the cattle when they got back home so he put it in the outside rumble seat. Shortly thereafter it started to rain so he brought the dog inside and put it on the shelf behind the seats. It was an extra burden to their travels, especially to Zelma on their honeymoon in a small car on a long trip. At her request, Stanley finally let the dog out of the car and they proceeded on their way. He later regretted what he had done and said, "I should not have picked up that dog." They returned from their honeymoon ready to begin their new lives together.

Chapter 2

The Family and Farming Years

"In every conceivable manner, the family is the link to our past, bridge to our future."
Alex Haley

During their family and farming years Zelma and Stanley had eight children and lived at six different locations as listed in sequential order below:

Overview of the Homes of Zelma and Stanley

1) 1929-36 Route 48 north of Englewood Children: Mary Ann, Lowell, Nancy, Linda Vocation: Dairy farmer with his dad, processing and delivering milk and dairy products
2) 1936-40 Marysville, 180 acres Children: Ron, Gary Vocation: Farmer
3) 1940 (three months) With Zelma's parents in Englewood Vocation: Plumber
4) 1940-44 Route 55 west of Troy, 10 acres Vocation: Farmer, Waco aircraft
5) 1944-45 Route 48 south of West Milton (Simmon's Place), 100 acres Children: Ted Vocation: Farmer
6) 1946-93 County Line Farm, 144 acres Children: Doug Vocation: Farmer, real estate, factory work, retiree

Stanley and Zelma were married the year the stock market crashed (1929). As the worst American economic depression began, they were fortunate to be in the farming business where Stanley could raise crops and animals that would supply their food needs. They both expressed how fortunate they were to be farmers at a time when so many people were out of work.

They discovered soon after marriage that they needed to be on their own where they could be independent of his parents who insisted on making decisions for them and even handling their finances. Therefore, they began making plans to get a farm of their own. They saved their money and Stanley cashed in his life insurance policy making it possible for them to obtain a 180 acre farm which included 20 acres of woods and a creek called Troublesome Run that ran through the farm. The farm was located 70 miles northeast of their original location in Union, Ohio where he had farmed with his dad. The farm was actually located between the small towns of Raymond and Peoria in Union County where Marysville was the county seat. It was always referred to by the family as the Marysville house.

Big Hickory Nut trees and wild rose bushes grew in the front yard at the Marysville farm. A crude outdoor fireplace provided the setting for many wiener and marshmallow roasts and a palace to play softball. A rope and tire swing hung from the branches of a tree and the children had fun cracking open the hickory nuts with rocks to eat the nuts. When they brought acorn caps to the supper table, Zelma would put a miniature treat under each cap as it was placed at each child's plate.

Life at Marysville was never boring. Zelma saw to it that both work and leisure were creative and enticing. The family maintained a large garden for food and to teach the value of work and living off the land. Every child who could hold a hoe was given a garden job. Zelma had a way of making it sound fun – rather like Tom Sawyer's logic to get the fence white washed.

Preserving and canning was another job. Apple sauce and green beans were always "put up" in half gallon jars. Garden spaghetti was a basic staple that was frequently served. It was a big yellow squash-like vegetable which was sliced, dipped in a milk and egg mixture, coated with crushed corn flakes then fried.

The array of activities for the children included making hollyhock dolls, dandelion chains, the game of Andy Over, rolling old tires around the barn lot, making bows and arrows, constructing two stringed instruments from corn stalks and learning to whistle with a blade of grass held between the thumbs. One fourth of July Stanley set off some firecrackers in the side yard while Zelma and the children watched the excitement from the porch. For birthday parties, Zelma wrote poems which held the clue to where the present could be found. Sometimes it was a ball of string that led to your gift.

Music and singing was a wondrous source of fun as Zelma gathered her children around the piano. They occasionally sang at church. The Marysville home was the place where Mary Ann received her first piano instructions from her mother. Zelma also gave lessons to Mickey, a neighbor girl. Her grandfather, Murray Blackwell, an American Indian could spin a wonderful story around the campfire.

The family had few possessions in Marysville. Mary Ann recalls that Zelma told her many years later of having only a single dime on which the family needed to survive for the next two weeks until the milk check arrived. Since the family had cows and chickens and a good supply of food from the garden, Zelma spent the dime on a cake of Ivory soap. Although she was never fussy about cleanliness, the children were always well groomed. Fitch's Shampoo and rainwater from the cistern followed by a vinegar rinse were the routine hair washing ingredients. Zelma was also the family barber for their children, Stanley and some of the grandchildren. Stanley said he never went to a barber after he was married. Zelma humorously told her family that she would be quite rich if she had charged them for haircuts. She even cut her own hair which was very curly and was always worn in a bun at the nap of her neck in the early years of their marriage.

The Marysville house was not modern but within a year after they moved in Zelma's father Fred, installed electricity. Stanley purchased a refrigerator and a tractor with a bank loan, but both had to be returned when there was no money to make the payments. Horses were used to farm the land. Fanny and Cal were solid workers but a frail white horse named Hot Shot became sick and was found dead in the woods beside the creek called Troublesome Run, a fitting name for the problems Stanley faced while farming at Marysville. Misfortune seemed to prevail with the meager resources and anemic dairy cattle. The herd of 20 cows became diseased and undernourished because the soil was poor and the crops did not do well. Stanley's dad hauled half the cattle to his farm near Union where good grazing pasture could be found to nourish the cattle. In spite of the difficult times, the family always had food on the table and a good supply of milk and eggs. A highlight at the Marysville farm was the installation of an indoor bathroom, one of the first in the area.

Visits from aunts, uncles, grandparents and cousins were eagerly anticipated in advance of their arrival. Once, Uncle Dale brought a softball and a bat and taught the children how to play round-town. When Uncle Gus visited, he made a hammock of barrel slats. The doctor was seldom visited at Marysville but Zelma always had common remedies in the medicine cabinet. There was Lysol diluted in a basin of warm water for cuts and bruises, Black Diamond Lineament and Bag Balm for bruises and aching muscles. Castoria was used for an upset stomach. Dr. Marsh was called to the house to deliver both Ron and Gary while the children were taken for a walk by visiting Grandparents. On their return home they would welcome a new baby brother.

The children remember happy times at Marysville, but these were no doubt stressful times for Zelma and Stanley, the parents of six children, trying to make a living and to establish an independent life. After living four years at the Marysville farm, Stanley and Zelma sold the farm. After a short three months stay with Zelma's parents in Englewood, they moved to a 10 acre farm on Route 55 west of Troy. The family had a few milk cows, some chickens and a dog. Stanley worked at nearby Waco Aircraft making gliders for use in World War II. An indoor bathroom was again installed at this house. Visits by relatives were always a pleasure. Uncle Gus was again creative and thoughtful as he made a swing for the children under the big maple tree.

While living on the Route 55 farm, certain food products were rationed by the government to support the needs of World War II. The family was once again fortunate to be living on a farm where some of their food supply was raised. Zelma was happy that she could help some of her relatives by giving them some extra food tokens that the family did not need so they could buy such food products as sugar and coffee during that time.

Zelma joined a neighborhood club, a group of rural farm women who met monthly for social time as well as doing various projects including the packing and shipping of homemade cookies, candy and personal items to relatives of members serving in the war. Zelma's brother, Emerson was serving in the Navy. Another time the women learned how to make articles of clothing. They made dress forms for one another with instructions from the local home demonstration agent. Masking tape would be layered over a thin knit, sleeveless top worn by one of the women, thus creating the exact form for each person. After a time the garment would become stiff with layers of tape and would be carefully cut up the back so it could be removed. Mary Ann remembers the forms sitting on the kitchen table awaiting assembly and mounting on a stand, each bearing the shape of one of the women from the neighborhood club.

The entire family enjoyed the activities provided by the Grange, a farm organization which met at Concord School near Troy. Zelma had some reservations about belonging to a secret organization but somehow overlooked that in order to allow the family to participate in some wholesome activities. Zelma also served as president of the Concord P.TA. She was concerned that her children receive a good education both academically and morally and her family was proud of her leadership in this organization.

On one occasion while preparing a carry-in meal, there were unexpected calamities with the food. The baked ham which she had prepared and temporarily put on the hood of the car was confiscated by the dog. To make matters worse, her lemon meringue pie was smashed when Lowell sat on it.

A spotless house was never a priority for Zelma; however she always wanted the place to be tidy when visitors came so she cleverly devised a plan. When there was a need for quick cleaning when visitors came, Zelma surveyed the cleaning needs in the living room and called out a number which meant the number of items a child had to pick up to make the living room presentable before the visitor arrived at the front door. The children could move with amazing speed and usually had the clutter removed before the guest walked through the front door.

Zelma's most creative way for getting the work done was the grab bag event which she started at the Route 55 home. It was an incentive plan with points earned for the completion of various tasks and points taken away when tasks were not done or as a penalty for misbehavior. A large chart was posted on the cellar door each week and the scoring was meticulously done. Each Saturday night the points were tallied and the family gathered as Zelma brought out a bushel basket full of packages with simple wrapping. Each was a gift that was labeled, suitable for a girl, worth 30, 50 or 65 points, suitable for Lowell etc. Each Saturday night was anxiously awaited throughout the week. It was a time of cashing in points for prizes. The prizes or gifts usually included things that the family needed anyway: shampoo, toothbrushes, combs, writing tablets and articles of clothing which Zelma made on the sewing machine. The fact that these gifts were earned with points and that they were gift wrapped made it a treasure.

Ron still remembers one of his grab bag gifts, a set of jacks and a red ball in a clear plastic package that had never been opened. The Saturday night festivities included homemade refreshments and entertainment. The children took turns at being in charge of these areas. Refreshments such as popcorn and lemonade were served. The entertainment included such games as Andy Over, Capture the Flag, Softball or Checkers. Lowell was known for making pancakes and serving them with powdered sugar and providing a softball game when it was his turn.

Zelma was fully in charge of promoting the grab bag as a big event and in so doing, the work ethic was being developed and the excitement of Saturday night rewards and activities made the program a success. The children did not question Zelma's point system as part of the weekly activity. This event included a theme song, "On a Saturday Night" which Zelma played on the piano as the family joyfully sang. See Appendix E for the musical transcription. Zelma always had a sewing machine where she did sewing repairs or sometimes made clothing for her family as well as curtains, pillow cases, etc. A few times she made clothing for weddings including a wedding dress and bride's maid dresses. When Ron was restoring his 1930 Model A Ford, she took pride in helping him upholster the seats and door panels with maroon corduroy material as well as a headliner in a black vinyl material which looked very fashionable. Doug was impressed with her sewing skills when she made a bathrobe for him. She also put patchwork on his Levi's and patched the canvass top of his Jeep.

Vacations and eating in a restaurant were luxuries that Zelma and Stanley could not afford during most of their child raising years. However, there were other entertaining things to do. The girls were delighted when they got to visit aunts and uncles in the summer and sometimes they would stay for a week. Visits from relatives were a treat. Occasionally the grandparents would take some of the children on trips with them. On some occasions Uncle Dale invited some of the children to go with him in his big semi-truck to deliver potatoes. He often bought ice cream cones for them making it even more special.

The cabinet radio provided many entertaining programs during the child raising years. Stanley bought a Victrola with many 78 RPM records at an auction in the late 1940s. It worked as long as it was cranked before each record was played and the needle was sharp. In 1952, the family got their first television.

Helping others was a priority for Zelma and Stanley whether it was a neighbor, relative or stranger. One summer day when the family was living on the Route 55 farm, two trainer planes collided and the pilots parachuted to safety in a nearby field. Stanley was one of the first helpers on the scene to assist the pilots. Homeless individuals sometimes traveled along Route 55. If they stopped for food, Zelma always fed them either on the back steps or the front porch swing. Ron recalls inviting his childhood friend over to play. Zelma made it special by serving snacks. It was her welcoming attitude that made a favorable impression with her own relatives as well as guests.

Easter and Christmas were favored holidays for the family. Easter eggs were colored and the children had the sure knowledge that the Easter bunny would hide them while they were sleeping. One Easter morning Gary remembers being told by Zelma that she "spotted the tail of the Easter Bunny as he disappeared around the corner of the house." Although the children looked, the bunny was never seen again. At Christmas the children decorated the tree with Christmas ornaments, some of which were homemade.

All of the children remember the humor of chasing flies out of the house. With the frequent coming and going of children in and out of the house, the flies had easy access when the door was opened. On hot summer days when the flies become so numerous, Zelma gave each child two tea tiles, one for each hand. Everyone would vigorously flap the tea tiles as they herded the flies to the door. It was Gary's job to swing the door open while the flies made their exit.

A major improvement project at the Route 55 house was that of constructing a basement under the house. Stanley hired a worker to help him shovel the dirt by hand from under the house. The basement was then cemented so Zelma could have a place to do the laundry and store food. The laundry consisted of a wringer washing machine and two rinse tubs. Washing usually took the entire day. There was also a small storage room in the cellar for canned vegetables, cured meat and fruit.

World War II was declared while the family lived at the Route 55 home. The older children vividly remember hearing Zelma tell them about this event and knowing the gravity of the situation simply by the serious tone of her voice. Although the war seemed far away, it was brought close to home when a son of one of the neighborhood club members was killed in action.

In 1945 the family moved to the farm on Route 48 just south of West Milton called the Simmon's Place. This farm had good soil for growing vegetables and crops, an apple orchard and a cherry tree. At harvest time the family sold apples as well as vegetables at the roadside stand at the end of the lane. Ted, the seventh child was born while the family lived there. He was Zelma's first child born in a hospital. When Ted was born, it was necessary to supply him with oxygen to enable sufficient breathing at birth. The family came to realize, the necessity of the hospital setting for Ted's birth since an oxygen tank would not have been available during a home birth.

It was at the Simmon's Place where Zelma, Stanley and the six children piled into the tan Plymouth to go to church. Upon arriving at church the family often walked in a few minutes late. The influence of the church on the lives of the children would be a respected part of their future lives and choice making. The children were urged to participate in church activities which included Sunday school class, camping, singing and youth events. When Zelma dressed for church she often wore a small felt hat held in place with a pin and a small black veil that came down on her forehead.

On the fourth of July 1946, the family moved to the 144 acre farm adjacent to the Simmon's Place and known as the County Line Farm. The farm included 10 acres of woods and a spring beside the house that constantly flowed with an abundant supply of water. Doug, the eighth child was born while the family lived there. When naming Doug, Zelma was influenced by the television news reporter, Douglas Edwards so his name became the first and middle name for Doug. The family lived for more than 47 years at this farm. It was from here that each of the eight children left for college, married and pursued careers of their own.

Uncle Gus again visited the family farm with his handyman skills. This time he made a rowboat and oars. The pond provided hours of delight for family and friends. The boys remember watching the frogs and skipping flat stones on the surface of the pond. One summer day, Ron dumped a bowl of goldfish in the pond. It was a surprise when he spotted them swimming under the thin ice in the winter

Soon after the family moved to the County Line Farm, Zelma and Stanley both made plans to make some changes to the land and farm buildings to accommodate their needs for a dairy farm. They also knew this would be the place where their children would grow up learning many life skills and develop interests, so the renovations began soon after the move. This included the installation of a bathroom in the house, a pond for boating and recreation, a tennis court, a silo, a hydraulic ram, the moving of several farm buildings to accommodate the animals and the removal of the 10 acres of woods with dynamite and tractor power. This provided additional farmland. All of these changes proved to accommodate the farming and recreation needs of the family. Both the land and the farm animals were very productive at this farm.

At the conclusion of these renovations, Stanley began building his airplane hangar and a runway with the help of his sons. He had a ready supply of poles from the honey locust trees in the woods as well as the lower 40 acres of the farm. Zelma was well aware of his flying interests before their marriage and she was happy to see him fulfill his dream of flying. Although all of his children flew with Stanley, Zelma never did. She did not feel safe in small airplanes. She said she felt more secure when flying in the larger commercial airlines.

It was during these years (the early 1950s) that Zelma's parents began to develop health concerns. Her father, Fred kept ferrets in a cage in his barn. He liked these playful pets but they required a clean environment and careful handling because they could bite. Fred was the victim of a ferret bit when he was caring for these animals and he contracted parasites. This eventually resulted in his hospitalization at the Good Samaritan Hospital in Dayton where he died at 75 years of age.

Shortly after Fred's death, Zelma's mother needed health care assistance so Zelma and her siblings hired a caretaker to provide for her needs in her own home. Soon after the caretaker was hired, Zelma stopped by to visit her mother and check on the caretaker. It was during this visit that she discovered the care taker abusing her mother. Zelma immediately stopped her from any further employment. Zelma and her siblings realized they had hired the wrong person to care for their mother. At that time they placed her in the Fairborn Rest Home where she received competent health care for the remainder of her life. She lived one year longer than Fred and died at the age of 79. Both of Zelma's parents were known for their kind and caring ways. Fred was an industrious entrepreneur as an electrician and Nora was proficient at the many household responsibilities and at growing flowers and vegetables.

The Bulldozer returned to the County Line Farm in 1964 to change the pond beside the lane to a creek and to enlarge the pond in the lower 40 acres for swimming and recreation. Doug and his friends added some features which increased the attractiveness of the pond. A rope was suspended from the sycamore tree for rope jumping into the pond and a raft was built from four 55 gallon barrels. A deck was constructed of redwood. It served as a platform from which to fish and swim as well as playing "King of the Mountain." During the winter the family and friends enjoyed ice skating and games of hockey on the pond

The pond was also stocked with bass and bluegill. A 14 inch bass was reported to be the record catch although larger fish were spotted but escaped being caught. The family had many picnics beside the pond and on one occasion the church used the pond for the baptism of several individuals as some of the church congregation gathered around the pond. Zelma was proud of these farm renovations and the many benefits they brought to family and friends. The family had the pleasure of many visitors for relaxation and social gatherings.

Many elm, cedar, beech and honey locust trees grew in the lower 40 acres. This area was also used for grazing cattle, sheep and hogs. The creek flowed through the center of the lower 40 acres where the family had a good supply of Christmas trees to choose from each winter. Watercress grew in abundance in the creek and the area was a habitat for many animals including rabbits, pheasants, raccoons, muskrats, red fox, weasels and many insects. During the winter months, the boys had the pleasure of trapping for muskrats along the creek and pond.

All of Zelma's children liked to participate in sports. On Sunday afternoons, the boys played football or softball games with the neighborhood boys in the pasture south of the house. Zelma encouraged her sons to engage in sports and occasionally came to see them participate in high school and college football and track and field events. They also played softball on the church softball team. Most of her sons were pole vaulters. A pole vaulting area was set up near the house where they practiced. A few years later when Doug was in high school, he excelled in pole vaulting. A more modern pole vaulting area with an asphalt runway was built beside the barn where he sharpened his skills at using the fiberglass pole. He went on to set a high school pole vaulting record. Later he received a scholarship to pole vault at Austin Peay University in Clarksville, Tennessee where he vaulted for four seasons.

Soon after moving to the County Line Farm, Zelma was involved in a service project with the ladies at the church. They met at Zelma's home and prepared boxes of food and personal necessities to send to relatives and others in need in Germany following World II. Many years later when Ron was engaged with his Brethren Volunteer Service assignment, he visited the Dorflingers, Zelma's cousins and one of the families who had received some of the supplies. It was a warm experience for Ron to meet them. They had remembered receiving the packages and shared their appreciation for the these gifts that Zelma and the church group had sent to them. However, they also said that the occupying forces helped themselves to the coffee and sugar before they received these gifts. Ron had the pleasure of visiting the Dorflingers several times. He noticed how similar cousin Genoviva and Grandma Nora looked, especially with high fat cheeks and soft skin. Zelma corresponded with the Dorflinger relatives frequently and later had the privilege of visiting them and their extended family in Germany when she made a trip to Europe with Stanley and their children, Linda and Doug.

Stanley bought Zelma's first piano from a family in Englewood shortly after their marriage. The same piano stayed with the family throughout the remainder of their lives. Music was always a highlight in Zelma's life and she played the piano often. In the early years at the County Line Farm Zelma organized a family percussion band. She played the piano as the children played a variety of homemade instruments using pots, pans, lids and spoons from the kitchen. In the early 1970s, Stanley took Mary Ann to a Dayton music store to help select an organ for Zelma's birthday. She continued playing the piano and organ all her life.

The family attended the West Milton Church of the Brethren throughout their years at the County Line Farm. Zelma strongly supported the churches position of volunteer service to assist people in need in such programs as Brethren Volunteer Service. She also served as pianist for the Junior Choir for a period of time. Sometimes she served on church committees. Zelma was known as a good and honest debater in Sunday School classes and although her views were sometimes opposed, she was highly regarded by those with differing opinions. She often liked to continue the discussion in the car on the way home from church. Doug recalls how Zelma took time to discuss world affairs as well as political and educational issues with him and she did not necessarily hold to family tradition as exemplified in the presidential election of 1960 when she voted for John F. Kennedy.

When Zelma and Virginia Hemmerich, a church friend, got together, it seemed to be a therapeutic outlet for both of them. They engaged in humor as well as serious discussion. Zelma found Virginia to be the kind of person who could accept her style of humor and return it in like fashion. During one of their whimsical moments she talked with Virginia about what heaven would be like. Zelma explained that she had a less literal interpretation than many in the church. She told Virginia, "When I pass through those pearly gates, I'm gonna' do flip flops down Main Street." Virginia's response was, "Now Zelma, I can see you doing that."

Humor was an anticipated element in Zelma's relationship with her close teaching colleagues, Margaret Harshbarger, Martha Crew and the school secretary Elizabeth Walker. One Halloween, Zelma and these ladies dressed up in men's clothes with suspenders and disguised themselves as older men. They went trick or treating in West Milton at the homes of some of the teaching staff including the principal, Oneida Minnich. After keeping the principal in suspense, they finally revealed their true identity. The principal enjoyed their antics and sense of humor.

Zelma was proud that Stanley was quite knowledgeable about dairy cattle, most of which were registered Guernsey cows. At various times he also had beef cattle, hogs, poultry, sheep, bees, and Shen the horse. Shen was a gift from Linda and Jim Biller. The major crops were corn, wheat, oats, hay and soybeans. He had a sparse supply of farm equipment to start with and it was usually second hand. His John Deere and Huber tractors both pulled two bottom plows. Eventually a Ford tractor was added.

During the dairy business at the County Line Farm, Stanley had as many as 26 milk cows at one time. His sons helped with the job of milking and caring for the cows. Since he had no milk cooler, he built a two-wheeled cart which was used for hauling cans of milk from the milk house to the spring house about 25 yards away. The cold water kept the milk cool until it was picked up the following day by the dairy truck driver. By 1947 Stanley had a room built adjacent to the milking house with a milk cooler installed. Automatic milking machines were purchased and the dairy business was up to date.

Everyone in the family had some part in helping with the farming responsibilities as they became old enough to do the work which included rounding up the cows for milking, feeding the cattle, washing the milking machines and returning the cattle to the pasture. Feeding hay and ensilage to the cattle was another daily job. Border collie dogs that were trained to herd the cattle. The first dog was Fritz. The next was Lady. Both were dependable workers. It was a pleasure to record the weight of the milk from high milk producers. The highest producers were Red and Pet. Both of them could fill the five gallon milk container to the top at each milking.

It was understood that radio music made the cows more content so they would produce more milk, therefore the cows got use to the routine of a radio playing while they were being milked. Zelma knew how demanding it was for her sons to get up before school, complete all the milking responsibilities then get to school on time and she often expressed her appreciation as did Stanley.

Zelma was the disciplinarian when raising her children. Her word was final when it came to proper behavior and her children respected her toughness at enforcing appropriate behavior. If the belt was necessary, it would not be spared. Profanity or saying a "bad word" was not tolerated. A bar of soap was used to wash the mouth of such an offender as she held the violator in a head lock.

Doug never experienced Zelma's mouth washing routine but he did remember the leverage she applied to get him to do various jobs at home. She would remind him of the hard work his brothers and sisters did and her pride in them. As her children became teenagers, she never set a time limit for them to be home. She trusted their judgement in coming home at a reasonable time. It was a feeling of mutual understanding that they would use common sense on this issue and her trust was respected by her children.

Her message of the harmful effects of smoking never came in the form of a lecture or rules on the subject. Rather it was her spoken values of mature judgement and wise choice making that she imparted to her children. During Lowell's high school years, she smelled cigarette smoke in his 1937 Chevrolet on a Saturday morning when he was out the night before with his friends. No matter who the smoker was, on that occasion her stern lecture tactic was sufficient for Lowell to heed her reprimand.

Nancy and Linda were baton twirlers in the high school band. Zelma believed that this activity would help them develop confidence and poise. They performed many sophisticated routines and often practiced in the front yard. They wore white boots and had lights on their batons for night time performances. It was an impressive routine at halftime with the lights out. Once they performed at a University of Dayton football game. They also went with the band to all of the high school basketball games. Zelma made their uniforms and on one occasion Zelma was still sewing the uniforms that Nancy and Linda needed for their performance at a basketball game that was in progress. Half time had arrived when Zelma finally rushed in with the uniforms. The girls, still nervous from the wait, were able perform in the nick of time as if there was no emergency. Zelma was known for her last minute jobs and her occasional late arrival for meetings.

For many years the house was heated by coal and even dry wood was brought to the basement to heat the house. Since the heat was never adequately piped upstairs, the upstairs bedrooms were always cold during the winter. Occasionally severe thunder or snow storms caused power outages. Doug explained that Zelma always made sure there were plenty of blankets and candles in glass holders to provide light at night. When there was no school due to weather conditions, she made use of the time by baking. She often served cookies and hot chocolate.

During the early years at the farm, the woods were a wondrous place for some adventures. There were large hanging vines for swinging, picnics, hunting, gathering raspberries, blackberries, sassafras and mushrooms. The family was able to take advantage of these experiences for several years before the woods were totally cleared for farming.

Lowell and Ron developed an interest in flying as a result of Stanley's flying career. Years later they would become private pilots and fly airplanes of their own. Zelma was proud that they were able to pursue their flying interests but she described flying like hanging in the sky with everything going by so slowly. She was also concerned about the dangers when flying a small airplane and on several occasions her fears were justified.

In the mid-1950s when Stanley flew his airplane to Canada on a fishing trip, Zelma received a phone call from him telling her that he had just crashed the Piper Cub. The accident occurred while he was flying low along a highway trying to read road signs. He was so low that his front wheels caught the electric wires between two poles which immediately brought the airplane down. Although the airplane was demolished, Stanley had the good fortune to escape this crash without injury. After salvaging the metal for $50.00, he came home on a bus. Zelma described how they both passed the crash site a few years later when they took a trip to Canada. The memories of the crash were so repulsive to Stanley that he could not look when Zelma drove past the area.

A few years later at 5:00 am when the family was still in bed, Mrs. Buehler, a neighbor who lived on the north side of the farm, drove in the lane at a high speed to inform our family that the hanger was on fire. To the horror of the family it was discovered that the entire building by now was absorbed in flames. It was too late to save anything. The hanger burned to the ground with Stanley's newly purchased Taylorcraft airplane inside the hanger. The fire was believed to have been triggered by the brush fire the evening before when Stanley and some of the family were burning away the dead debris that surrounded the chicken house which was adjacent to the hanger. There were probably traces of smoldering dry grass that had drifted toward the hanger during the night. Some property insurance helped but it was still a painful loss. As the family helplessly watched the hanger burn to the ground, Stanley told Zelma, "This is the end of my flying career." Within another year the hanger was rebuilt at the same site and Stanley bought another airplane. In all of Stanley's major purchases (airplanes, cattle, vehicles) he always included Zelma on the decision. Accordingly, this provided comfort for her. For smaller farm sale purchases there was no consultation. Sometimes these purchases were questioned by Zelma.

Stanley's next airplane was a Vagabond which he flew for about one year before selling it to purchase a Cessna 140. He enjoyed flying this more versatile airplane for many years. One of his flights was to visit Ron and Evonne when they were living in Connecticut. His longest trip was a flight to Los Angles where he visited Gary. He then flew to Oregon before taking a northern route home.

One day he took off from the County Line Farm while Zelma stood in the yard and watched. She saw him lift off the runway heading south. She explained how he was gaining altitude as he reached the hanger and was over the south field. Shortly thereafter she heard the engine sputter and eventually stall. She then saw the airplane go down and crash in the neighbor's field, the property of Bob Mitchell. She immediately ran in the house and summoned the paramedics. The airplane was totally demolished but this time Stanley did not escape without injuries. He received some broken ribs and ankle bones as well as a compound fracture above the ankle that would present walking problems for the rest of his life. At that time, Stanley was on his way to a nearby airport to fill up with gasoline. He knew his tank was low but thought he had enough gasoline to reach his destination for a fill up.

The smell of a fresh cut Christmas tree in the house was a highlight for the family and there were plenty of them in the lower 40 acres. Zelma engaged the children in decorating the tree and the house at Christmas time. She sometimes made white divinity, chocolate fudge, peanut brittle and baked goods. She also supplied the family with the rare treat of tangerines and nuts. When she had time she liked to make Christmas presents on the sewing machine. One time she formed a Christmas tree from candied popcorn with gum drops on the outside for Mary Ann to give to her school bus driver. During the Christmas season Zelma played Christmas songs on the piano and sometimes read a few stories like "The Night before Christmas." She would also tell the younger children how Santa was going to enter the house and put presents under the tree. It was the younger children's job to leave a snack for Santa to eat. When the younger children awoke in the morning, she continued the story by telling them that she "heard noises last night that sounded like Santa was here." Upon showing them the apple core and an empty coke bottle, she confidently showed them evidence that Santa had come.

Getting something new even if it was used was a momentous occasion for the family. Some of the new items were: Lowell's first two wheeler bicycle, the traditional wrist watch, a high school graduation gift, a basketball, Lowell's collarless sport coat that Zelma had sewn for him and the dogs,

The children were aware that the family could not afford to buy many things but they also knew that they would always have a lifetime supply of milk, eggs and a variety of packaged meats and poultry to choose from in the large three door deep freezer in the backroom. Earl Sleppy, the butcher was called on to kill a steer and prepare the meat whenever the deep freezer needed more meat.

Zelma was in charge of the sale of eggs. Since there were more eggs than the family could use, an "Eggs for Sale" sign was posted at the end of the lane. Zelma also took eggs to Englewood where they were sold at her parent's home. The family also sold milk to a dairy processing company. The trucker who picked up the milk also had ice cream which the family often purchased. In the early years at the farm Zelma purchased bread from a bakery who delivered bread products to their customers in a van.

Throughout their child raising years, Zelma and Stanley as well as their children were fortunate to have good health other than some allergies and the common cold. Zelma was allergic to penicillin and sulfa drugs, so she used other antibiotics. She had serious breathing problems whenever she was the victim of a bee sting. It was frightening to her when a bee got too close, so the bee hives were located on the east side of the hanger. They provided the family with a good supply of honey. Zelma helped her children when she could in their various 4-H and F.F.A. projects throughout their high school years. Mary Ann, Nancy and Linda developed homemaking skills which remained useful throughout their lives. Zelma encouraged the development of these skills and went to the county fair to see their projects.

Zelma was known as a good cook with fried chicken, potatoes and gravy, liver and onions, pork chops, sweet corn and many casseroles. Her desserts were a treat: black bottom pudding, pineapple upside down cake, angel food cake, cranberry sauce with black walnuts and berry pies. Left over pie dough was buttered and sprinkled with sugar and cinnamon, then baked into pastries. Sometimes she was known to leave food in the oven, toaster or skillet too long and it was over baked or burned too much to eat. On hot summer days Zelma or Stanley served a watermelon that had cooled in the spring water. Homemade ice cream was a frequent treat in the summer time. It was cranked by the children in the two gallon freezer. Zelma's tasty ice cream recipe was still used by her children years later. Evening snacks sometimes included popcorn or apples.

Leisure activities in the evenings included games like Rook, Pit, Chinese Checkers, Scrabble and Monopoly. With her skill as a wordsmith, Zelma was often the winner at Scrabble and other word games. Playing cards was considered a game of gamblers, so a deck of the usual 52 cards was not seen in the house for many years.

Zelma and Stanley always had a large truck patch where a variety of vegetables were planted each year. The many jobs involved from planting to harvesting or canning became family projects. On one occasion Zelma had the children shell peas on the front porch. The flies became so numerous that she gave each child towels to wear as headscarves to keep the flies away, but it was a strange sight on a hot summer day. The non-ending job pea shelling gave Ron the idea to improve the system, He suggested shelling the peas by putting the pea pods through the washing machine wringers where the double rollers would automatically shell the peas and they would be collected in the washing machine tub below. Upon putting this plan into practice only a small percentage of the peas were recovered as most of them shot in random directions, even with the umbrella fastened to the top of the washing machine to direct the peas into the washer tub. On one occasion when Gary was putting peas through the wringer his hand got caught between the two rollers and was pulling his arm through. Fortunately, Ron came to the rescue just as the wringer had pulled his arm all the way to his shoulder.

Gary witnessed a bizarre incident with the yellow 1937 Studebaker pick-up truck that could have been more alarming than it was. Zelma was dressed up to go shopping in West Milton. She was even wearing a fur coat that day. Lowell was going to drive her by way of the back lane by taking the runway to Baker Road. The pick-up had low seats that were made of slick plastic material and the doors would never shut securely. They were opened from the inside by leaning your shoulder into the door. It had just finished raining hard and there was a large puddle of water covering nearly the entire barn yard area with water two to three inches deep. Lowell had just started pulling away with Zelma on the passenger side. He continued to increase his speed as he was going through the big puddle. When he rounded the corner by the double corn crib, the door on Zelma's side flew open. Zelma slid out the door and into the large puddle of water. As she fell out the door, she managed to grab the running board of the truck with one hand and hold tightly as she was drug another 20 feet through the mud before Lowell brought the truck to a stop. By that time Zelma was covered in mud and her clothes were ruined. Lowell got out of the truck and ran back to get her as she was lying face up in the mud, panting and exhausted from the strenuous and shocking ordeal. As he tried to raise her up at the shoulders, she did not have the strength to talk but eventually told him between gasps for air to, "Just let me rest." She did recover as she lay in the mud puddle for a few minutes and was later helped to the house. As for the door, it was never fixed but it was well-known, when using the yellow Studebaker pick-up truck, user beware!

Sometimes Zelma took the side of her children in questionable situations as happened in the chicken episode. Ron was in the habit of driving Lowell's green 1937 Chevy to school at the age of 14 after he and Gary finished milking the cows. Ron has since wondered why Zelma and Stanley allowed him to drive to school without a driver's license. He believes it was a trade off as a favor to him for doing the early morning milking responsibilities before school, especially since no one had to taxi him for his after school activities. Ron was known for expediency when driving. On this particular morning he was again driving to school the back way with Gary, his passenger when they came upon a large flock of chickens pecking for food in the middle of Mote Road, a gravel surfaced road. Ron was already well over the speed limit, but he didn't want to be late for school. Gary was thinking he would eventually slow down, but that never happened. Ron drove through the middle of the flock of chickens. After the initial thumping and bumping both boys looked back and saw nothing but feathers. Ron's instructions to Gary were, "Don't tell Mom." Ron recalled entering his homeroom as the tardy bell was ringing. Upon taking his seat, he looked out the window and noticed the Chevy conspicuously displaying a clump of white feathers on the grill. Later when Zelma did hear the story, she refrained from disciplining Ron, but said, "I wonder why that farmer let his chickens out on the road anyway."

In the late 1950s, a good friend of Zelma, Iris, gave her the gift of a porcelain rooster figurine which she called Iristotle. This gift would be the beginning of Zelma's collection of roosters in various forms of wood, stitchery, metal, ceramic, glass and resin. She originally displayed them on shelves in the living room. When she received more than the shelves could hold she moved them to some longer shelves in the dining room. She was proud of the artistic and colorful array of roosters. They were all gifts to her from relatives and friends. Many were from countries around the world. During her later years, she asked her children and extended family to choose a few roosters for themselves. These personal gifts prompted memories and conversation about Zelma.

Zelma's muscles were unusually flexible. She could flex into positions that even astonished her children. When asked she would show her children how far she could flex. With arms held straight overhead she would bend forward at the waist and touch the floor with the palms of her hands while keeping her legs straight. On some occasions when asked, she even had a friendly wrestling bout with Stanley where she held him to the floor for a few seconds. Stanley cooperated and said, "I don't want to hurt her." Doug recalled that Zelma also wrestled him during his junior high years. She was able to win by combining strength and humor. On the way home from church one time, Zelma bet Stanley that she could beat him in a foot race to the end of the runway and back. With Doug as the referee the walk/run race ended with Stanley clearly the winner. Both were good sports and Zelma was proud of her attempt.

Zelma and Stanley took two extended vacations with Ted and Doug when the boys were very young. The first was to Florida in the late 1950s where they visited Sarasota, Cyprus Gardens and some church friends. In 1961 Stanley and Zelma vacationed with Ted and Doug again in some of the western states including a visit with Jim and Linda who were living in Miami, Arizona. Doug recalls some of the highlights of the trip were seeing Grand Canyon and Old Tucson as well as Jim and Linda and the open pit copper mine where Jim worked. The hotels were inexpensive or sometimes it was a sleeping bag in a park, but Doug described it as a fun adventure for them and a delightful visit with Jim and Linda.

Zelma had a commanding vision that writing, story-telling and expression through poetry carried the potency to stimulate many positive values. Therefore she would take whatever time and wordsmith maneuvering was necessary to express her thoughts. She also took time to personalize her letters to individuals or to a more general audience as needed. When she wrote her poems and stories, she would sit at the old Smith Corona typewriter and gaze away to compose her thoughts. She was so engrossed in her writing that she would tell Doug, "Why don't you take a hike? Go to the creek with Lady (the dog)."

When the children left home for their various careers, Zelma did some creative things with her writing. She wrote farm news and stories word for word as dictated by Doug with her occasional prompt and embellishment to enrich the story. At that time Doug was in the early stages of language development. Accordingly, her unusual literary form gave the reader the flavor of what was happening on the farm plus the humor of hearing it told by their younger brother. Doug enjoyed the recognition and opportunity to express himself and those who received the letter felt connected with the family back home.

Zelma's advice in essay or speech writing was a boost to her children during their high school years. When Ron wrote a prize winning essay in high school, he recognized Zelma's helpful council. Ron's topic was, "My duty to God and Country." Zelma and Stanley both proudly attended the high school assembly to see Ron receive the American Legion sponsored award which included a trip to Washington D.C. where he visited with his congressman as well as various monuments and memorials in and around the Washington D.C. area. Doug noted that Zelma seldom monitored his homework, but she offered more than helpful advice when he had writing assignments. On some occasions she even wrote portions of his paper for him.

She gave great thought to her children when they were overseas and her typewriter put her closer to them. She proudly kept a map of the world posted on the kitchen bulletin board to pinpoint the location of her children. Doug therefore developed a love of geography and writing as did all of her children. As her children grew into adulthood, they all contributed their personal writing skills and memoirs at family gatherings which have been saved by each child.

Story telling was another of Zelma's competencies. She sometimes read bedtime stories to her children. Ron and Gary remember how she would bring Brer Fox and Uncle Remus to life with her animated vocal enunciations. Doug has memories of sitting on the bedroom floor listening to her read, Houdini the Handcuff King, Blondin, Wizard of the Tightrope' and The City that Died to Live (Pompeii).

Zelma saw a college education as necessary for all of her children. She encouraged them to attend a Christian college, especially Manchester since it was the family's church college and it is where she attended. However, she would have favored any college that suited their needs. Her advice to the girls was, "You need college to support your family in case your husband dies." Zelma and Stanley supported their vocational desires, whatever they chose to do. They furthermore expressed their pride in their chosen field of work. Their children prepared for and worked in the following vocations:

Mary Ann attended Manchester College, continued her piano studies and established herself in a piano teaching career throughout her life. She also served as organist and sometimes choir director at her church. She organized many musical presentations at various venues including the Troy Hayner Cultural Center in Troy, Ohio.

Lowell was educated at Manchester College and Ohio State University. He pursued a career with the Bureau of Employment Services where he helped people secure job training and employment.

Nancy attended Manchester College before becoming a registered x-ray technician and radiologist through studies at Good Samaritan Hospital in Dayton, Ohio. She is also certified in the treatment of cancer patients with radiation therapy.

Linda attended Manchester College before becoming a registered nurse (RN) at Grant Hospital School of Nursing in Columbus, Ohio. She then earned a bachelor of science degree in nursing at Indiana University of Pennsylvania where she graduated cum laude. She is also a certified diabetes educator.

Ron earned a BA degree in history at Manchester College and an MA in social work at the University of Connecticut. He did doctoral studies in public administration at Florida State University before taking a career in the administration of criminal justice in the states of Wisconsin, Connecticut and Ohio. Later he established his own business and became a general contractor in home construction.

Gary earned a BA degree in physical education at Manchester College followed by an MA in elementary education from California State University and a doctorate of education at the University of Oregon. His vocations were elementary teacher, secondary special education teacher, school administrator and university special education instructor. Later he wrote several published books on the subjects of biography, poetry and autism.

Ted graduated from Manchester College in three years with a BA in psychology and sociology. He earned his MA in social work from Florida State University. Ted was a volunteer agriculturalist in Di Linh, Vietnam when he was killed by forces opposing the American military as he began his third year of volunteer work. His life as a courageous peace hero is permanently celebrated at the Dayton International Peace Museum, university peace walls, Milton Union High School Hall of Honor, the Annual Ted Studebaker Academic and Athletic Achievement Award at his high school, tree dedications, books, and CDs of music.

Doug received an athletic scholarship to Austin Peay University in Clarksville, Tennessee where he pole vaulted on the track and field team for four years. He graduated from Austin Peay with a BS and U.C.L.A with an MSW and MBA. His careers have been in the fields of developmental disabilities, home health care, hospice and employee counseling programs. Later he cofounded and managed an interior design and home furnishing business. He then established an Airbnb hospitality business.

All eight children of Zelma and Stanley were attracted to social service vocations. When Zelma was asked, what the toughest part of being a mother was, she replied, "To let my kids go and do what they want to do." She quickly added, "Of course, no one wanted to rob a bank so I was safe there."
One summer a neighbor who lived nearby on the County Line Road, hung himself with a rope in his barn. Ron remembers going to Zelma with many questions as to why someone would do something like that to himself. She discussed this catastrophe at length with Ron and expressed that he must have felt very poorly about himself. She went on to emphasize the importance of talking to people as well as listening to them, feeling good about yourself and doing what you know is right. She was always very disturbed that tragedies such as these happen with no one detecting such an occurrence in the developmental stages and rescuing the person ahead of time.

Zelma's detailed letters to her children at college gave them fulfillment as well as a sense of belonging. When they came home she would stay up late into the night talking to them regarding their thoughts and concerns about college. She was a good listener and there seemed to be nothing more important than the thoughts of her loved ones. Ron remembers Zelma's help with a very difficult decision process he was going through as he was deciding what to do with the upcoming choice of military service or alternative service. He remembered her reassuring advice that no matter what his choice, his family and the church would be supportive in whatever decision he made.

Zelma did not see it as her role to interfere with decision making in the lives of her married children. She had a firm awareness of appropriate rapport among the family as well as with others. She said the most enjoyable part of life for her was to see her family have some happiness and for them to make the world a better place. Wherever their careers, marriage and service assignments took them, it was fulfilling for her to visit or stay in communication with them if only to be encouraging. She advised that you should not expect life to be smooth and easy because we learn best as we go through the difficult parts of life. She compared it to climbing a mountain. She said, "The only mountain that is climbable is the one that has sharp edges and a rough surface where you can get a foothold." She emphasized that life's problems should be used as a stepping stone for learning.

When her children were going through difficulties, she said she felt the pain but knew that intrusion would be futile and inappropriate. She knew her role was to listen and support. Some of the difficult times for her as she thought about her children and extended family were divorce, behavioral disorders, early deaths, medical conditions and home destruction due to a fire.

Zelma had deep feelings about the need for equality and non-discriminating practices in all areas of life. In her own way, she wanted to take a stand on these issues. On August 27, 1963 she traveled on a bus to attend the "March on Washington for Jobs and Freedom" with Verda Mae Peters, a relative and church friend. They participated in this enormous civil rights event to advocate for jobs and freedom (See Appendix B, Zelma's program and notes). Joining this march was not a popular thing to do for some people during that period of time. Verda Mae even received threatening phone calls due to her intent to join the march. In Washington D.C., Zelma and Verda Mae joined the huge throng of marchers which stretched from the Washington Monument to the Lincoln Memorial. She proudly supported this event where she saw and heard many of our nation's civil rights leaders speak or sing at the podium in front of the Lincoln Memorial including Martin Luther King Jr. as he gave his historic, "I Have a Dream" speech. She noted how urgent yet peaceful the demonstrators were. As she was traveling home on the bus it was her feeling that the impact of this event would be long remembered in the history of our nation. She believed this event would be a step toward shaping decision making for equality. Gary also attended the same event having traveled to Washington D.C. from Maryland where he was in training for his International Voluntary Service assignment. Gary and Zelma did not see one another at this event as these were the days before cell phones. However, they later spoke to one another about the significance of this event which continues to be a prominent civil rights landmark.

Zelma came from a conservative background, yet over the years she became even more aware of and interested in cultural cooperation. Her children's friendships, travels and social exchanges added to her appreciation for humanitarian values..

Card playing and dancing were not accepted activities in her Mennonite background. Yet as an adult, these were not issues. Rather, her focus was on the bigger picture of finding ways to improve the quality of life for all. She took pride in the pen pal letter exchanges between her third grade class and a group of Laotian students when Gary worked in Laos. On another occasion when Gary brought a middle eastern fellow student home from Manchester College and he chose to not go to church with the family on Sunday morning, Zelma understood the cultural differences and was fine with his belief. She took an interest in talking with him and learning about his country and Muslim beliefs. On several occasions when Bob Buhl, Doug's father-in-law visited at the County Line Farm, Zelma always made sure ash trays were available in the house for him to use. Regardless of her personal beliefs a welcome was always a priority over such values and practices that were different than hers.

Four of Zelma's children left home to pursue service assignments of their own in foreign countries (Germany, Morocco, Laos and Vietnam) for military service, Brethren Volunteer Service, International Voluntary Service and Vietnam Christian Service. She explained that each time her son's departed for a foreign assignment she felt like she was making the journey with them. She was concerned about their safety as she realized there would be times that they would be in harm's way. After opening a letter that Lowell had written to her from Fort Knox, she wept as Lowell explained how one of the Army recruits was killed in a tank accident. Soon after Ron had arrived in Morocco, he was carrying out a survey which required riding a mule to reach people in a rural mountainous area. As he dismounted the mule he was riding, the mule bit him at the elbow and began swinging him back and forth off the ground as Ron tried to escape. After a few days of hospitalization, Ron received a letter from Zelma. She described in her letter that while washing dishes one morning, she heard him yelling, "Mom, Mom." Then she realized that Ron had departed for Morocco three months earlier. She then wrote a letter to Ron describing the incident and how bizarre she felt writing such a letter. Ron received that letter in Morocco one week later. By the date on the letter, he realized she had written the letter on the exact day that he had the encounter with the mule. Ron's friends who witnessed the incident informed Ron that indeed he had yelled the words, "Mom, Mom" while he was being assaulted by the mule. Ron described Zelma as having "more than a mother's intuition. This was a clairvoyant encounter but seldom did she let it be known."

Gary recalls talking to Zelma as he was packing his bags before he departed for his volunteer agriculture assignment in Laos. They were both aware that a civil war was being fought in that country, yet volunteer service outweighed his desire to do nothing or seek an assignment elsewhere. He commented to her before departing. "If I'm killed over there, I have the satisfaction of knowing that I had the privilege of participating in life including volunteer service in Laos." She knew that also, but her return comment with broken words was, "You're not going to be killed."

When Ted accepted the assignment to serve in Vietnam during the war, she was well aware that he was going into harm's way, as was Ted and the whole family. She knew of the possibility that he may not return.

On the morning of April 27, 1971, Stanley and Zelma received the most shocking news of their lives, that their son, Ted had been killed by soldiers opposing the American troops. It happened when Ted's house was attacked with a mortar barrage. He was 25 years of age and had just started his third year of volunteer service with Vietnam Christian Service. Knowing that Ted would not return home brought Zelma's deepest moments of sorrow. She realized that three older sons had previously served overseas for two years and each had returned home safely.

Within a few hours of Ted's death, all the children had gathered at the farm from their homes across the country. They had come together to support one another, to plan a memorial and to begin to deal with the traumatic loss of their brother. They knew that they were a tight knit family. This incident simply reinforced that bond. Later Zelma described her thoughts to her immediate family:

> "After a brief period of time, the others all left the room for other parts of
> the house or to work outside and I was left sitting alone. My heart was so
> full of pain and my head full of thoughts any mother would think. How can I
> let go of him? He's in God's hands now, beginning his eternal life."

At about the same time Zelma described to her family how she saw a red and black stripped butterfly appear briefly in the window shortly after Ted's death. She realized that this was a signal to her that Ted's life is secure in God's hands. Later when the mailman delivered Ted's guitar home from Vietnam, she wept at his huge sacrifice.

During the time of Ted's death, Zelma commented, "I feel fortunate that God gave Ted to us even if it was for a short time." It was because of Zelma's faith in God, that she could rest in the scripture promises and not carry bitterness with her about the loss of her son. She openly cited God's word as her basis for forgiving the person responsible in her son's death. She was proud of the peacemaking heritage Ted had forever established. Zelma spoke about Ted as a peacemaker when she was invited, on two occasions, first at the West Milton Church of the Brethren and later with Pakdy at the annual meeting of the Mennonite Central Committee in Chicago.

When Ron and Evonne were living in Cheshire Connecticut, Zelma visited them. Ron was assistant superintendent of the state reformatory. He asked Zelma if she would like to go into the prison and briefly talk to the inmates about herself and her family and get them to do the same. Although she was hesitant about the visit, she said she would like to do that. She spoke to them about many things including her life and her family, Ted's story and the struggles that followed. They asked her many questions and after about two hours, Ron had to pry her away from the inmates. The men were fascinated with her openness and sense of humor. They spoke of her for months thereafter and Zelma often asked about them in letters to Ron and Evonne and expressed her desire to do some form of volunteer work in a similar setting.

Ted's wife Pakdy came to Ohio at the time of Ted's death and stayed at the home of Ted's parents for a few years as she dealt with her devastating loss as well as cultural adjustments. At the same time she was trying to decide what to do with her life. Zelma described their talks as a much needed outlet in her life. She said, "Our relationship did something to ease the terrible heartbreak that seemed to be getting more and more agonizing as the days for me became more empty." She added, "I get tremendous comfort and satisfaction from talking to her (Pakdy) over and over." She also provided guidance and encouragement to Pakdy.

The memorial service was held at the West Milton Church of the Brethren. The following day the immediate family held a memorial service at the farm beside the spring and the willow tree. With Pastor Phillip Bradley presiding, the family scattered Ted's ashes beside the spring and sang "Blowing in the Wind." This occasion provided vivid images that remained forever with Ted's family.

Among the many local and national news reports was the ABC news team that came to the farm to gather information for their telecast. Zelma told how Ted's unselfish life of doing what he believed can impact society. She reported he died for the values he was raised with from his family, his church and in the Bible. When introducing Ted's story, Jim Kincaid, the reporter stated, "Ted Studebaker was a young man who told his draft board that he could not conscientiously accept military service, but that he was perfectly willing to go to Vietnam." The telecast went on to describe Ted's marriage of one week before the tragedy to Pakdy, a Chinese volunteer from Hong Kong and his martyrdom. In a local newspaper article, Keith Weidner, Ted's high school English teacher said of him, "He gave all he had to give. Small wonder, I feel diminished." Zelma experienced many deep emotions as she realized the impact of Ted's stand for humanity.

A few months before Ted was killed, Howard Royer visited Ted in Di Linh and described Ted's life and work for peace on several occasions. At the 25th year after Ted's death, Howard wrote, "What a memory for the church to celebrate and cherish, and by which to be encouraged and empowered." Ted's immediate family members continue to hear stories from persons whose lives were affected in a powerful way for peace and justice after learning about Ted's life. Joel Freedman was one of Ted's Florida State University classmates in the social work program. As a writer in upstate New York. Joel has written periodic news articles about Ted's humanitarian life.

Besides many news and curriculum articles written about Ted, his life continues to be celebrated at the following venues:

Published books:
- Moore, Joy Hofacker. Ted Studebaker. A Man who Loved Peace. Eugene, OR: Wipf and Stock Publishers, 2017.
- Studebaker, Gary W. and Douglas E. Studebaker. Ted Allen Studebaker, An Enduring Force for Peace. Eugene, OR: Wipf and Stock, 2017.

Museum display:
- A permanent interactive display at the Dayton International Peace Museum

Peace Wall inscriptions:
- Gladys Muir Peace Wall at Manchester University, North Manchester Indiana
- The Lion and the Lamb Peace Arts Center, Bluffton University, Bluffton, Ohio

Tree Dedications
- Tree dedications at the County Line Farm and in Di Linh, Vietnam

Courtyard inscription
- "Ted Studebaker Our Peace Hero," at the Bethany Theological Seminary

Published music CDs
- "Ted Studebaker in Vietnam" produced by Steve Engle
- " Heroes and Friends" produced by Tim Kearns

Milton-Union High School Awards
- Hall of Honor Award, Peacemaker
- Annual Ted Studebaker M Trophy Award presented to the graduating senior displaying highest achievement in academics and athletics

If Zelma kept a grandma's brag book, it would have contained many spellbinding stories. It is no secret that upon hearing her talk or write about her children, grandchildren and in-laws, there was sometimes a touch of exaggeration woven into her comments. After Phyllis Cribby, a family friend read a news report about Gary; she turned to him and remarked, "I didn't know you taught Buddhist Monks when you were in Laos!" Gary responded, "I didn't know that either."

Evonne described Zelma as the lively one when she, Ron and Zelma were in San Francisco. Even after the exhausting drive from Los Angeles, she insisted that Ron and Evonne "go out on the town, hit a few night spots and have some fun." She was going to be alright at the motel. As it turned out, Zelma was the last one to turn in after staying up late talking to Ron.

Doug's wife, Linda described how accommodating Zelma was during a visit she and Doug were having at the farm. Stanley was preparing to take them to the Darke County Fair. He was in a hurry to get an early morning start, even before they had a chance to eat breakfast. As he was waiting in the car parked in the driveway, Doug and Linda went out to get in the car. Before they left however, Zelma hurried out to the car with a tray filled with breakfast for them, complete with scrambled eggs, bacon, eggs, toast, coffee and orange juice. Linda expected to have breakfast sometime that morning, but not the convenience of having it delivered to the car to eat en route to the Darke County Fair.

On another occasion Zelma came to the rescue of Gary and Sue. They had visited the farm as part of their honeymoon excursion. They were awakened early one morning by the thundering sound of a 12 gauge shotgun outside their bedroom window. They later discovered that Stanley was trying to get rid of a large flock of sparrows that had gathered in the maple trees in the front yard. He was successful in driving the birds away but not without being reprimanded by Zelma for the early morning wake up call to the guests on their honeymoon.

Zelma occasionally did substitute teaching in the elementary schools in West Milton. Eventually she and some of her teaching friends accepted teaching jobs at Huber Heights, southeast of West Milton. Her fulltime teaching career brought about many positive changes in her life. She developed a wide range of teacher friends as well as enormous satisfaction in her teaching vocation. She was experienced with the development of children and felt good about her teaching abilities. School administrators were aware of her background and depth of teaching experiences but she needed approximately two more years of college courses to complete her degree and teaching credential. At the age of 53 she enrolled at Miami University to complete her college work. Some of her courses were at nearby locations but most of her courses were 60 miles from home at the Miami University campus at Oxford, Ohio. One day a week, Zelma and two of her teaching friends, Maude Henderson and Hazel Doles traveled together to Miami University to complete courses toward their teaching credential.

She was a good student and enjoyed the companionship of the ladies when she made these trips with her friends. Although she needed two courses per year to keep her job, she picked up the pace and increased her work load of courses. She was proud to be engaged in the class discussions as well as the written assignments. Her persistence and goal oriented style were evident considering the 120 mile round trip she made once per week at the end of her teaching day. In 1968 at the age of 61, she graduated from Miami University with a Bachelor of Science degree in education (see Appendix C). It was an honor for her to participate in her graduation ceremonies and when she received her degree with family members present, the university president acknowledged her enormous accomplishment. The entire family was extremely proud of her at the achievement of an early childhood goal.

Zelma taught third grade students for most of her teaching career. She was a very respected teacher. One of her specialties was teaching her students to be good writers. She had a routine established with her students. Every morning they were given the assignment of writing for 10 minutes on a topic of their choice. She told them it could be about their experiences, hopes, dreams, difficulties, questions, discoveries, family life, etc. She also had a large repertoire of topics that she would assign for journal writing experiences. She had such a talent for teaching writing to young children that she was invited to Wright State University on two occasions to share her expertise by speaking to students who were preparing for careers in elementary education.

The Ohio law requires teachers to retire at 70 years of age. That is when Zelma retired after having a very fulfilling teaching career of 19 years. She was honored by the staff and parents at her school, Valley Forge, as her teaching career ended on a very happy note. She was honored by the school's Parent Teacher Organization for her dedication to the children as well as her teaching skill (see Appendix D). At Zelma's retirement, she and Stanley were able to do some things that they had in mind for a long time. They vacationed to several different locations (Europe, Alaska and Hawaii), visited their children, lived in their Florida home during the winter months and enjoyed more leisure time.

The winter of 1978 brought the most severe snow storm ever to hit the County Line Farm. At that time Stanley and Zelma were living by themselves on the farm. The snow blizzard and cold weather continued for many days and they found themselves snowbound and concerned for their survival. The high snow drifts in the lane as well as the County Line Road and other major roads made vehicle travel impossible. Furthermore, the basic necessities for survival were being eliminated by the snow storm. They were able to call for help on the telephone but they had no electricity and the oil furnace was inoperable making it as cold in the house as it was outside. Zelma described how they huddled together in the living room to stay warm, hoping for an end of the snow storm. Knowing that Stanley and Zelma were stranded in freezing weather with no heat, Lowell and cousin, Jim Studebaker and some of Jim's son's towed a heating generator on a sled from Paul Studebaker's home to the home of Stanley and Zelma, about three miles away. It was towed by Lowell's tractor most of the way, until the tractor could not get through the snow drifts. Then they pulled the heating unit on a sled which was quite strenuous, through the snow drifts. They finally reach Stanley and Zelma with the heating unit after battling the wind and snow drifts.

Hope had arrived at last for which Stanley and Zelma were grateful. The storm had subsided, but this horrendous episode confirmed their thoughts that this would be the last winter they would spend at the Ohio farm. They were now thinking about enjoying some retirement years in a warmer climate.

Chapter 3

The Florida Years

"...the most important aspect of family history is preserving a record of the present for the future."

Guy Black

The winter storm of 1978 prompted Zelma and Stanley to begin looking for a warmer climate. Shortly after the storm ended, they traveled to Florida in search of a winter home. They found a home they liked in Lake Placid, Florida, purchased the home and made plans for moving to Florida the following winter when it would be ready. In 1979 Stanley and Zelma spent their first winter at their Lake Placid home. It was a two bedroom dwelling with citrus trees in the yard surrounding the house and lots of space and plant life between houses.

Stanley welcomed the pleasure of making friends, fishing at the nearby lake and taking care of the citrus trees on their property. It was an adventure for Zelma to take trips with Stanley to places of interest in Florida. She also continued reading, letter writing and playing the organ which they brought from Ohio. Zelma was delighted to provide organ music. It was relaxing for Stanley to listen to the songs that Zelma played. He often sang along.

They had many friends who were already living in the Sebring, Lake Placid area and were pleased with the many relatives and friends who visited them. Two of their granddaughters also lived in Florida so Zelma and Stanley enjoyed visiting with them. Amy lived in the Tampa area and Jill lived in Jacksonville.

After living in Lake Placid for four and one-half years, they sold their home and moved sixteen miles north to Leisure Acres, a mobile home retirement community in Sebring, Florida. They wanted to make this move because it was closer to their friends, their church, shopping and services in Sebring. This new environment also eliminated the work required to maintain their Lake Placid home and property. At Leisure Acres Stanley and Zelma had the privilege of selecting their activity preferences from many choices. Zelma maintained a calendar to schedule and record the functions they chose to attend. She became involved in arts and crafts. Together they attended club house travelogue programs and some social events. Zelma began riding a three-wheeled bicycle to get some exercise. They also participated in bus trips to various cultural performances such as the Florida State Fair in Tampa, a dinner and theater performance at Lake Wales and Cypress Gardens, a botanical garden and theme park near Winter Haven. Stanley had many friends with whom he enjoyed playing pool. He often prevailed over many of his friends as well as his own relatives who visited them in Florida.

Shortly after they moved to Sebring, Stanley's brother Dale and his wife, Marilla moved from Ohio to a retirement community in Lake Placid, Florida where they bought a home. Zelma and Stanley had many happy times visiting with Dale and Marilla and eating out together.

Their life in Florida provided an appreciation for the freedom of travel, new and uplifting encounters and the well-deserved pride at being able to have these enriching leisure opportunities at retirement. They traveled back to Ohio during the summer seasons and a few times during the winter to celebrate Christmas with their family. This change alone provided them with the attraction of the farm, family and friends.

Having good health and the means to enjoy leisure time in Florida was a wondrous period of time for Zelma and Stanley. Their children looked on with pride as their parents experienced this retirement adventure in Florida. It was a well-deserved reward for their diligent work and productive lives. It was also the Florida years that added another exciting chapter to their lives.

June 14, 1979 marked the 50th wedding anniversary for Zelma and Stanley. Their children, spouses and extended family were present at this gala celebration. The activities included a visit to a photography studio for a session of family photos, a hog roast beside the pond where their son, Doug and grandson, Craig roasted a hog overnight, and where a large picnic with swimming and volleyball were part of the celebration the next day. Zelma and Stanley were again honored during the morning church service at the West Milton Church of the Brethren where many friends and relatives came to an open house luncheon and celebration in the afternoon.

A dinner was held at Mary Ann and Milton's home where 50th wedding anniversary gifts were presented to them including a quilt. The quilt contained block designs contributed by their children, spouses and grandchildren. Each block's design was a reminder to Zelma and Stanley of each member of their extended family. It contained the contributor's name and an embroidered anniversary greeting or design. The blocks were sent to Linda, their daughter who pieced them into a double bed size arrangement. They were then hand quilted by Cynthia Studebaker. It was a very attractive quilt with historical significance. Zelma and Stanley were surprised and honored to receive this one-of-a-kind gift, realizing the large amount of work completed so many relatives. Listed on the graph below are the contributors to the quilt with their greeting or design:

The 50th Wedding Anniversary Quilt

Name, relation to Zelma	Quilt block design
Milton Milton, son-in-law	Two fish. "I fell hook, line and sinker for your first and landed her at last."
Mary Ann Cornell, daughter	Piano keyboard. "You gave me the keys to happiness."
Julia Lutz, granddaughter	A butterfly. "Having grandparents like you is better than a silver nixley or a golden wally wally. Love you." (This was an expression that Zelma had coined)
Craig Huffaker, grandson	A red haired skier sitting on top of a toilet waving a trombone and a pipe wrench.
Cindy Huffaker, daughter-in-law	Girls skating on the Studebaker pond, skiing in Colorado and playing tennis.
Jill Morris, granddaughter	Florida sunrise.
Zachary and Joshua Martin, great grandsons	Baseball, bat, cap and teddy bear.
Ted Martin, grandson-in-law	U.S. Navy ship and patriotic eagle emblem.
Brad Huffaker, Grandson	Trombone and tuba. "Sound the brass for 50 years!" (music teacher)
Brian Huffaker, grandson	Guitar with "Ohio State" on it. A flower pot with two blooming flower faces. "I'm pickin' you two late bloomers to never grow old." (landscaper)
Amy Powell, granddaughter	An open book inscribed, "In the general ledger, you're my capital account. Studebaker and Roth in business for 50 years." (accountant)
Lowell Studebaker, son	Detailed picture of his home, winding driveway and bridge over the stream and trees.
Diane Gillespie, granddaughter	Dove. "The Holy Spirit in the form of a dove."
Dan Studebaker, grandson	A square balanced on top of a triangle depicting the delicate balance of relationships.
Dave Studebaker, grandson	Chicken house at farm with a crowing rooster on the roof, sun in the horizon and a small airplane circling overhead.
Nancy Smith, daughter	Skeleton with red heart symbolizing Nancy, the x-ray tech.
Alison Bucchi, granddaughter	Butterfly with the inscription, "Madam Butterfly." (a name Zelma gave to Alison)
Phil Smith, grandson	A sack of penny candy from Jay's and a soccer ball.
Linda Post, daughter	Sewing machine and nursing cap with hypodermic needle. "Sew happy to be your TLC."
Jim Biller, son-in-law	Pick and shovel. (mining engineer)
Jenny Sprecher, granddaughter	Farm scene with house, porch, willow tree and Jenny riding her horse.
Jim S. Biller, grandson	An after dark scene at the farm with Jimmy and his cousin, Phil being spooked by Grandma as they ran for the house,

Name	Quilt block design
Ron Studebaker, son	Airplane flying in three clouds: white (1929), silver (1954), and gold (1979). "May your spirits soar and fly as the clouds and years pass by. May you feel free of harm, twixt Lake Placid and the farm."
Evonne Studebaker, daughter-in-law	White dove with olive branch and burning candle. "May you always go forth in peace, love and light."
Ranya Studebaker, granddaughter	Ballerina on her toes. "May you be blessed by beauty all around."
Tarik Studebaker, grandson	Baseball, bat and glove. "May play make you happier."
Kendra Sherman, granddaughter	"I love you when you always tied my shoe, lifted and carried me when I was two. Grandpa and Grandma, I love you."
Chad Studebaker, grandson	Tractor and animals. "May your roosters always be crowing and your fields always growing."
Gary Studebaker, son	Guitar
Susan Studebaker, daughter-in-law	State of California.
Ramona Studebaker, granddaughter	Palm Tree.
Pakdy Studebaker, daughter-in-law	Red butterfly. "Life is Great!"
Doug Studebaker, son	Skier.

Chapter 4

Grandchildren

"The greatest legacy one can pass on to one's children and grandchildren is not money or other material things accumulated in one's life, but rather a legacy of character and faith."

Billy Graham

Julie Lutz

I remember Mom (Mary Ann) and Dad (Keith) loading us six kids in the station wagon and going to Grandma and Grandpa's house via Route 55 to Calumet to 48 to the County Line Road to their long lane. Their farm was one of my favorite places to go because I got to spend the night. I remember waking up to roosters crowing. Most of the time I hung out with Grandma because Grandpa and my uncles (Ron, Gary, Ted and Doug) were always busy doing farm work and really didn't want a little girl tagging along.

Zelma always had fun, creative things to do and she always seemed to enjoy my company. She would take me on nature walks. We lay on a blanket outside at night and observed the stars, made stencils out of potatoes and lots of other activities. She would let me sort through her button box and pick out my favorite buttons. I loved to go to the grocery and Five and Dime stores with her. I even got to see Grandma in action in her third grade classroom at West Milton because Troy had a different spring break schedule.

Sometimes Doug would let Craig and me play up in the hayloft where we made a maze with bales of hay. We would play tag. I also remember Uncle Doug racing us around the house. He would even give us a head start and still win. He raced barefoot around the house once when it was snowing. I also remember Uncle Doug telling us to pinch him as hard as we could in the stomach because he was tough. Usually when he did that, Grandma would sit on him and make him say "Uncle."

I remember fresh eggs and fresh milk (which I did not like). Uncle Ted tried to teach me how to milk a cow. I was afraid I would hurt the cow if I squeezed and pulled as hard as he insisted so this "city girl" never did learn how to milk a cow.

Sometimes Grandma took me to Uncle Doug's wrestling meets. If I remember right, he pinned everyone he wrestled. Grandma always had a candy bar for him before the match because he claimed it gave him a spirt of energy. She always had one for me too. She also had Kleenex ready for Doug because he would get so worked up before each match and sometimes cry.

I remember a lot of little things:

- Grandma was so flexible that she could bend at the waist while keeping her legs straight then put her palms flat on the floor.
- Athletic competition between uncles on the living room floor at the farm.
- Grandma playing the piano and organ.
- Hollyhocks in the side yard by the clothesline.
- Going to the old West Milton church with Grandma always wearing a hat.
- Drinking cold water down at the spring.
- Picnics in the yard and down by the spring.
- Grandma collecting roosters. I remember attempting to count all the roosters in her house. I stopped when I got to 500. She had wallpaper with roosters and three big rooster lamps and dishes with roosters.
- Grandma told me once she would often go skinny dipping down at the pond on hot nights. I have yet to find someone who has witnessed this.
- The only time I remember getting in trouble at Grandma and Grandpa's house was when I ran over the sweeper cord with the sweeper and broke it, but Grandma came to my rescue.
- Christmas at the farm. Lots of relatives, food and presents. I recall the first time I got to sit at the "big people's table" and listen to their storytelling and reminiscing.

I think Grandma knew everything there was to know about kids. At different times in my life, Grandma wrote a note or letter to me that would bring a smile to my face and joy to my heart. She had a way with words. She is the person I most want to be like. I will always love and miss her.

Craig Huffaker

Funny thing, all of my memories of Zelma are good ones. I guess that says it all because she was a good person. She had the uncanny ability to see good in everyone and accentuate the good she saw in everybody she met.

Some good memories:

- Going to the farm and getting my haircut. Always a sensitive subject with me but always fun when Grandma did it.
- There was the time when Doug got hold of the electric razor and put a permanent scar in my head.
- Ice skating on the pond in the winter and trying to stay up with the uncles playing hockey. It seemed like there were a hundred pairs of ice skates in the back closet. Upon returning to the house after skating Grandma served good hot chocolate.
- Having Doug try a new wrestling move on me, screaming at the top of my lungs and Grandma rescuing me by pulling him off and sitting on him. She didn't need any fancy wrestling moves to pin Doug.
- Picnics at the farm were great. Grandpa Stanley would fire up the barbecue and throw some hot dogs on. Always burned them so they were real good. Watermelon staying

cold in the spring at just the right temperature for eating. And of course, homemade ice cream the old fashion way with a manual crank.

- Swimming in the pond. Jumping off the rope from the old sycamore tree and diving off the old raft made of redwood boards and 50 gallon metal drums.
- Digging for worms beneath the piles of cow dung below the pond and fishing.
- Having a pig roast with Doug and all our friends. Spending the night by the pond cooking the pig. In the morning Grandpa got up and made what all my friends dubbed "special sauce" (barbeque sauce) for the pig. It was delicious!
- Christmas at the farm. When I was probably 8 or 9 I asked for a play gun so I would have a real gun when I played army with my friends. I was certain Grandma was going to get it for me, but she didn't. As much as I was disappointed then I still remember this and her obvious conviction for peace. To this day I have never owned a gun nor have I been in a fight. A lesson and belief that I learned from my Mom and Grandma for which I remain thankful.
- A final thing I will remember about Grandma is her strong conviction for unconditional love. She placed no conditions on you for receiving her love. I hope I can be this way.

Jill Morris and family

- I remember lying under the willow trees with Diane and Grandma telling stories.
- Watching the clouds go by with Grandma while she explained what each cloud looked like.
- The smell of the farmhouse, picking strawberries and swimming in the pond.
- Grandma and Grandpa in Florida. Zach and Josh trucking around behind Grandpa picking up fruit that had fallen on the ground.
- Spending Christmas with Grandma and Grandpa at Lake Placid which was nice since the rest of the family was so far away.
- Grandma working with Zach to cool his tantrums. She would very cheerfully take the screaming Zach to the bedroom and shut him in. Then she would sit on the floor on the other side of the door and talk softly. Eventually Zach would want to hear what she was saying, so he would stop wailing, then Grandma would open the door and a hugging, more pliable Zach would pop out and give "loves" to Great Grandma.
- The duck weathervane that Joshua loved so much at the end of the drive at the Lake Placid home.
- Long walks and three-wheeled bike rides.
- Zach and Josh playing pool with Grandpa.
- Excellent home cooked meals, even if they were fattening.

Brian Huffaker and Family

- Blake remembers that Grandma liked tapioca. One time he made some and took it to her at The Home.
- Kate remembers that Grandma collected roosters from around the world. She gave Kate two. One was made of glass with many different colors.
- Kate and Blake remember giving Grandma a stuffed rooster at The Home. Because her vision had failed, she felt the gift until she figured out what it was. Once she figured it

out, she sang a "chicky" song and crowed like a rooster, putting her hands up to her mouth like a megaphone.

- Ann remembers when Grandma and Mary Ann came over to the apartment to see how her wedding dress fit. Grandma checked the hem from the landing.
- Brian remembers getting haircuts with a razor. Brad and I use to get burr haircuts and Grandma would really whack it off. She could get pretty gruesome with the scissors. We certainly didn't come out looking like we did when we came in. In retrospect, I sure did appreciate having a cooler head in the summer than I would have otherwise.
- Swimming at the pond. I probably have three pairs of glasses resting at the bottom of the pond. I would always forget to take them off before I swung out on the rope for my descent into the water. I often tried to dive and recover them, but to no avail. They were buried at the pond.

Brad Huffaker

The many memories that occurred at the farm have been covered by my siblings, so I'll concentrate on the time since I left Ohio. Since 1982, I've received over 20 letters from Grandma keeping me well apprised of the activities back in Ohio. I've kept them all. Her writing ability was clearly top notch and a letter from her was always newsworthy and supportive. Particularly nice was her letter writing exchange with the fourth grade students where my roommate was teaching. The students sure learned a lot about those "Gringo" up north from that letter writing exchange with her "entire" family. I received a particularly supportive letter from her at one very low point in my life which I will never forget. She was the only person who understood the situation fully and her support strengthened my decision. I think about this often and am eternally grateful for her support.

There are several incidents that I remember from late in life. One time, when she was staying at my parent's home, Grandma, Doug, Linda and I were playing Scrabble. I spelled the word "rood" not knowing whether or not it was a word (something I often do in that game). Doug, of course, immediately challenged the word, while Grandma came to my defense. As Doug was looking up the word, Grandma leaned over to me and said. "Sure rood is a word. That's what the rooster does to the hen if you know what I mean." I laughed so hard I hit the ground.

During this same visit from Doug and Linda, we were eating on the deck out back. There was one particular Monarch Butterfly that kept landing on Grandma's shoulder. At that time in August, the Monarchs were making their trek back to Mexico, but this particular butterfly was enamored with Grandma because every time she shooed it away, it came back and sat on Grandma's shoulder. It did this at least five times. I think the butterfly wanted to take Grandma with him but we wouldn't let him! At least the Butterfly knew where to land.

I remember being chased around the barnyard to get those famous burr haircuts as a kid. So I asked her to cut my hair when her vision was failing. She asked me if I was sure and I told her to go ahead. She butchered it, but I can say I was the last person who ever got a haircut from Grandma. By the way, I didn't get a burr and I fixed it later.

My last recollection does not involve Grandma directly, but rather Grandpa. I visited him once when he was living at the farm by himself. He was in a particularly cantankerous mood (when wasn't he?). He wanted me to drive him to the bank in Englewood. Once there, he proceeded to try to fix me up with a bank employee which was typical for him. On the way back to the farm he talked about all of his girlfriends. Once we got to the farm he asked me to drive diagonally across the field. The corn was three feet at the time. I tried to talk him out of smashing the corn with the car but my efforts were futile. As we drove out smashing the corn, he said all along that he got the girl of his dreams, Grandma. How fortunate for all of us.

Amy Powell

I have so many memories of Grandma it is hard to know where to begin. My earliest memories are on the farm. I remember:
- Stringing and snipping beans
- Picking berries by the silo.
- Getting toys out of the kitchen bench where all the goodies were kept.
- Being afraid of the horse, Shen. One of the cousins would lure him into the barn with a carrot and another would shut the door behind him so that we could go safely and freely back and forth to the pond.
- Grandma teaching me how to cool off on a hot day. I was to put my wrists under the cold spring water. She said that cooling off your wrists, cooled your whole body. I believed that it worked and it did. Grandma made everything seem possible.
- Running to Grandma to be safe from Grandpa when he caught me playing with the buttons on his electric orange massaging recliner.
- Grandma's messy kitchen cupboards and cleaning them out for her once. I don't think she liked it but she never said anything but kind words to me for doing it.
- Opening Christmas presents one at a time from youngest to oldest. I thought it was a good idea until more cousins were born and I had to wait longer to open mine.
- Grandma playing the piano and organ as I would sing along to some of her favorite hymns, Amazing Grace in particular.
- Alison and I making Brownies. We decided that the batter was so good that we ate it all. Grandma had another box of Brownie mix in the cupboard so I got it out made another batch while we continued to eat the one we had just made. Grandma was outside the whole time so we thought she would never know. Alison and I both began to feel sick before we got through all the batter. We mixed what was left in with the new batch we had made. Grandma never said that she knew, but I believe that she did. Maybe the chocolate all around our mouths was a giveaway.
- Grandma setting all her presents from students out on a table for the grandchildren to weed through and take what they wanted. I always thought she was crazy to give away such treasures. But now that I teach, I'm anxious to have children and grandchildren to give my treasures to as well.
- Making dandelion necklaces.
- Grandma having silly sayings and rattling off silly poems.
- Swimming and ice skating on the pond.
- Walking down the airplane runway when all the corn was tall and feeling like I was in a secret passage way. I would make my way down to the back road on a hot day and then start popping tar bubbles on Baker Road.

- When a girlfriend and I rode our bicycle from Troy to Grandma's house, we would stop at the river at Calumet Road and eat lunch. Then we would continue on. When we finally arrived, Grandma would have some cold drink ready for us. We would stay the night and head back the next day.
- Playing in the hay loft with the cousins.
- One time Phil, Dave and Jimmy made a "secret" potion and tried to get us girls (Alison, Jenny and me) to drink it. We never did, thank goodness. The boys told us later that they had urinated in it.
- Driving Grandma and Grandpa to Florida one year. Grandpa had a urinal (like you get in a hospital) behind the driver's seat in the car. I spied it before we left the farm and asked him about it. He said it would save time from having to take pit stops. I assured him that I would stop wherever he needed. He still insisted that he be allowed to bring it. Grandma and I told him it was ok, but only if it traveled in the trunk. On the way down, he wanted to use it. Since we had to stop to get it out of the trunk anyway, we just went to the rest area where we could use the facilities. He then realized that this was our plan all along. We also had a tire problem along the way. They had just purchased a Pontian Catalina. After the noise got so bad and the ride was so bumpy I convinced Grandpa that we had to stop at a service station. He was convinced that they would "rip us off" but Grandma insisted that we stop and I was driving so I followed her advice. It was a good thing we did. All four tires were about to blow. They had been put on wrong. We replaced all four tires then headed on to Florida. Uncle Lowell called the place where they purchased the car and was able to get their money reimbursed for the tires.

  When it was time to stop for the night, Grandpa was to pick the spot. There like a beacon to any true blue Studebaker was the sign he had been waiting for, $19.98 per night, continental breakfast included, free. We pulled into the parking lot and were blinded by all the flashing neon lights. Grandma and I were not thrilled, but Grandpa was out of the car with his bag. Grandma told me to leave him so we could go to some place more respectable. I half thought she meant it but I couldn't just leave him there even if part of me didn't want to see what the inside of one of these rooms looked like. Grandpa got the room and we went in. It wasn't much but it did look relatively clean. I also learned what a loud snore Grandpa has. Between the noise and the flashing neon lights outside the window, I didn't get much sleep. The next morning at our free continental breakfast, Grandpa reminded all of us of the great deal we were getting. Grandma said, "Yep, for worn out beds, flashing lights, stale donuts and strong coffee, we sure got a deal," in a very sarcastic tone. On that note we departed. I was glad we had only one night's sleep over on our way down.

- One time when we played the word game, Boggle, Grandpa used the word, "ted." Grandma said he couldn't use it because it was a proper noun. We all know that Grandma is a word expert or at least that is what I believed. Grandpa stood his ground. He said he was right and put it in a sentence, "He will ted the hay." Grandma said that he may have told Ted to bail the hay. After much discussion, I finally broke out the dictionary even though I knew Grandma was going to be right. But my eyes could not believe the description on that page, "ted... to get the hay." There was something

Grandma didn't know. I was amazed. Grandpa walked around tall the rest of the weekend, using the word "ted" whenever he could. I know that he hadn't been able to stump Grandma too often so he was going to play it for all it was worth. Grandma was a very good sport about it all.

- Riding the motorcycle down to visit them thinking I was never going to make it because my behind was so sore. I called Grandma at the half way point and told her that I had to give my bottom a rest. When I finally arrived she had a hot bath waiting for me.
- Picking fruit from the fruit trees for breakfast.
- Grandpa coming home from an auction with a frame from a lawn chair with no webbing on it and wheels at the bottom. Grandma and I were sitting on the porch when he came home. When he pulled it out of the trunk, I started to laugh but Grandma didn't so I stopped. Grandpa brought it over and was so proud of his big find. He said, "Guess how much I paid for this?" Grandma replied, "If you paid more than a penny, you paid too much." Grandpa seemed a little crushed because he had paid a quarter. He then explained that he got it for Grandma to put the laundry basket on so she could wheel the clothes to the close line. Grandma finally chuckled a little bit, then she put a basket on it and to our surprise it worked!
- Grandpa buying her an automatic washer for her birthday, just what he always wanted.
- Grandma and Grandpa coming to stay with me after my car accident in Tampa. It was at Christmas time and Grandma was the perfect caretaker. We were getting ready for dinner but the tablecloth was covered with crumbs so Grandma told Grandpa to take it outside and shake it. My apartment was on the third floor and my front door opened into a nice carpeted indoor stairway but my backdoor lead straight to an outside balcony. We assumed he would take it to the back and shake it, but before we could say anything, he shook all the crumbs in the carpeted hallway. Having them at that difficult time made my Christmas much brighter. Grandma and I made an angel for the top of my tree. It was made out of a toilet paper roll, Kleenex, gold paint and a yellow ribbon.

Diane Gillespie

My thoughts of Grandma are not so much of specific incidents, but rather of a profound Christian witness of self-sacrifice of serving others and God. Grandma was deeply affirming of me and contributed immensely to my sense of self-worth. She could make me feel like I was the only person on the planet, as she gave her undivided attention to me. She never complained to me about her lot in life but made the best of her situation. I had a dream of her that was so real that I was surprised to wake up. We were walking while having a conversation (in heaven I think). I know she's in heaven now entertaining the angels.

Dan Studebaker

The letters she sent while I was away at college and serving in the U.S. Navy really demonstrated what Grandma was all about. These letters were filled with confidence building, encouragement and support. She would always say those things that we all need to hear but never had the courage to say to others. In addition to her great pride in her large family, her faith was so strong and genuine that none of us could doubt that there was a God in heaven and that He loved us all.

Specific memories are kind of hard to conjure up, but I can remember some incidents pretty clearly from my childhood days and visits to the farm. For instance, I remember one day when Uncle Doug held me down, broke wind on my head and then ran out the front screen door of the house with Grandma right on his tail, yelling, "Douglas Studebaker!" I later passed this tradition on with my younger brother Dave being the unfortunate victim.

I remember the day we boys were swimming down at the pond when we heard Grandpa take off in his airplane. I turned and looked up to see the plane lift off over the road and then disappear from view with a pounding crash following a split second later. We ran to the house with our bare feet stinging from the dried weeds in the pasture and then the hot gravel of the driveway. We were scared to death as we burst through the front door into the house. There we saw Grandma; seemingly calm and collected speaking to the emergency rescue squad on the telephone and giving clear orderly directions to the site of the crash. It impressed me that she had probably rehearsed this inevitable event many times in her mind before. I suspect at that moment she believed Grandpa to be dead. Although she must certainly have been horrified, at the moment her actions and instincts shifted toward handling the situation in an orderly manner and calming us kids. I certainly knew then why I had never known Grandma to fly with Grandpa.

I remember riding in the car with Grandma many times as a child. Grandma always had a big car with lots of horsepower. I remember in particular, her big brown Pontiac Catalina. She wasn't shy about putting the hammer down. While Dave and I lived with our dad after our family broke up, Grandma did a lot of kind and gracious things for us. She dropped by almost every week with something to eat. Sometimes it was a pot roast, a pie or a cake. Whatever it was, we were sure glad to have it, as the weekly cuisine food left much to be desired. With the food was always a kind word or positive comment which she seemed to know we needed. And she was right! Grandma had a particularly strong influence on me when it came to education. She took great pride in her profession of teaching and her exceptional accomplishment of graduating from Miami University very late in life. Years later I remember noting the perfect grammar and exceptional quality of her letters I received from her while I was a student at Miami University. English was always my best subject, of which I'm sure Grandma was a strong influence.

As a youngster, I wasn't perceptive enough to realize and appreciate the great sacrifices Grandma made for the sake of her family and the burdens she endured. It was only in the later years of her life that I came to appreciate the difficulties she had endured and how she had always put the best face on some bad situations. When back pain, eye problems and a host of other physical ailments began to attack Grandma in the later years, she always seemed to rise above it. She didn't complain and usually wouldn't even admit to being in pain or discomfort. She truly loved life and was determined to not let anything stop her from living it. There's no doubt in my mind that Grandma had a profound and lasting effect on my life and that influence will live on and enrich the lives of my children. I am very grateful to her.

Dave Studebaker

Some of my best memories of Grandma are things like never leaving there hungry, whether it was a meal or a snack she had made for us or being filled with candy from the candy drawer we kids supposedly knew nothing about. Grandma wasn't that dumb was she? The drawer always had plenty in it.

She was always there when I was sick with a remedy or a pat on the back. It meant everything in the world just knowing that she was just down the road. Grandma would come to the pond lots of times and watch us swim. I can't remember how many times I've swung out on that rope; it was so many.

I remember the time when Jimmy, Phil and I were playing on the redwood raft which was anchored at the shallow end of the pond. Grandma and Pakdy were down there watching us. We had a mud fight on the raft and in the water where we pulled up handfuls of mud and slung it at one another. It was easy to pull up big globs of soft mud from the shallow end and we just splattered one another. We were eventually covered from head to toe with mud and were slipping and sliding off the raft. "King of the Mountain" was another favorite. We played this game at the deep end of the pond. Six or eight of us would try to see who of us could stay on the raft without being pushed off. Grandma would often bring food down to the pond and we would have picnics. I also remember the times we would play on the ice. Doug would throw buckets of water on the ice to make it smooth for skating.

Grandma also gave me jobs to do like painting the garage and fixing the dents in her car. I remember her reading stories to us and she never lost her knack for writing. She taught me a lot about writing. She would write post cards to me. I'll always remember her letting me help grade her student's papers. It seemed she always found a way to include the grandkids in everything.

Alison Bucchi

I recall the farm as a place of great fun and adventure:

- When I was very young we lived out of state but we always came home for the holidays. Christmas was a big production. Each person sat on the piano bench and opened their presents in the middle of the room.
- The way Grandma bounced as she played the piano when we sang Christmas carols.
- Grandpa had a movie camera for a few years and its bright light would momentarily blind each of us as he would zoom the camera all over the room.
- The adults would sit at one table and the kids at another. It was an important day when I was invited to sit with the adults.
- Watching the boys play hockey and seeing the back hall closet filled with ice skates.
- Listening to my aunts and uncles tell fabulous stories about their childhood. No matter how many years I heard them, I loved to hear them again and I still do.
- Grandma was always bustling around doing so many things, but whenever stories were being told or a child had something to say or show her, she always listened with intense interest. She made you feel important.

56

- When I was in the third grade we moved to Ohio and I visited more often. I was instructed to not ask for cookies when we visited Grandma and Grandpa, but of course I did. I'd stand behind her and whisper, "Do you have any cookies?' Then she would say out of the blue, "Alison, there are some cookies in the breadbox. Why don't you go get some?"
- Grandma always called me Madam Butterfly. I'm not sure why she did but I liked it.
- Uncle Ted and Uncle Gary walked on their hands on the sidewalk and up the porch steps in the front yard.
- One time Grandpa trimmed Shen's hooves with a hammer and chisel, not too successfully.
- Uncle Doug would ride Shen into the pond. My dad always said the warm spots in the water were where the horse relieved himself.
- Shen chewed a hole through our wool blanket to eat our picnic lunch so strategically hidden from him down at the pond.
- Walking out the runway with Amy to Baker Road and pop tar bubbles on the pavement on a hot summer day.
- Working hard to catch tadpoles in the pond. I had a whole jar full and had to go to the bathroom. Mom told me to go behind a tree and I wouldn't. I headed up to the house, started to climb the gate, dropped my jar and broke it. I cried and peed all over my tadpoles.
- Airplane rides with uncles.
- Thinking the pond was so far from the house.
- The rose arbor at the end of the sidewalk beside the spring.
- A wedding dress hanging in the upstairs hall closet.
- Grandma's very well done hamburgers.
- Grandma taught me the words to the song "Lightly Row."
   "Baby bye, here's a fly, let us watch him you and I.
    Up the wall, he does crawl, yet he never falls.
    I believe with six such legs, you and I could walk on eggs.
    There he goes on his toes, tickling baby's nose."
- Visiting Grandma and Grandpa in Florida with Brad and Brian and seeing a neighbor kill a huge rattlesnake in their back yard.
- Grandpa making breakfast at 4:00 am and Grandma taking us on a tour and to a shop where she made some crocheted dolls to sell.
- When I went to college, Grandma would send the most uplifting letters. I'd read them over and over. They were always humorous and told a story or taught a lesson.
- Grandma inspired me to get into education. She always had such positive things to say about her classroom experiences. She gave me some of her teaching visual aids and I gladly introduced them to my class. Later I had one of my classes read poetry on tape and sent it to her.
- Grandma made everyone feel welcome and loved whether they were a family member or not. My husband felt comfortable calling her Grandma.
- At the Brethren Retirement Community, Grandma was always happy to see us. My daughter, Whitney, three years old at the time, would rub lotion on Grandma's feet. We'd sing nursery rhymes and other songs together.

- I truly feel blessed to have such beautiful grandparents and a special farm to allow me to have a storybook childhood.

Phil Smith

One time in the middle of the summer, Dave, Jim and I decided that we were going to go for a swim. We were the three musketeers whenever we got together and we always managed to get a cut or scratch or something. As usual, we hadn't brought a suit with us. We often wore Doug's old clothes he left behind, but since there weren't any of those left, we decided to strip ourselves naked. It was especially fun when you went off the rope because you had to protect the precious jewels when you hit the water otherwise they wouldn't be so precious afterward. We were all swimming and when we looked up, down from the farm came Grandma and Pakdy. I don't remember if we were all in the water, but if we weren't, we all got in the water darn quick. We hide behind the raft hoping they would walk past and not notice us, but they saw us and came down for a visit. They had also brought down a large pan of beans to snip. They decided that they would snip and watch us swim. As it turned out, we didn't do much swimming, we watched them snip beans instead. We shriveled up into about nothing, but we felt fortunate not to receive any turtle or snake bites. I don't think we ever told Grandma about this either.

I rarely remember Grandma scolding one of her grandchildren, but I do remember one time. That was when one of the smaller grandkids wrote with a marker on a drum that Ted had sent back from Vietnam. I was so shocked that Grandma had actually scolded someone. I was probably about 14 at the time.

There were lots of memories at the farm. They included climbing in the hayloft, tooling through all the barns, the hanger and out buildings looking for trouble, swimming, skating and riding Shen the horse. There are a million stories related to Shen. He did not like to be ridden. While we were on, he would go as close to a tree as he could so that our legs were in danger of being pinched off between his belly and the tree trunk. We usually rode bareback, mainly because we didn't know how to put the saddle on. We were lucky to get the halter on. He would intentionally run under the clothesline, trying to hang you on it as he went under. He did this of his own accord as he knew where the clothesline was. When we would ride Shen down the road, he would stick his rear-end out in the middle of the road and would walk almost sideways. Once when Jimmy and I rode Shen, he decided that he was sick of us, so he started to lay down. We knew it was coming so we jumped off just before he hit the ground and ran to the car for safety. We weren't sure if the horse could get in the car to get us, so we locked the car doors to be safe.

I remember rummaging through all the stuff in the chicken house. There was always a treasure in there that we could play with. The trash pit was a great place to play because there were all kinds of glass and bottles. We would grab them and smash them all. Scope bottles were the best. But once there was an old TV in the pit. We had a contest, which I won. The award was having the privilege of throwing the first rock through the TV screen. It was like being able to carry the Olympic torch.

One time when we were in our 20s, Jim had a double barrel shotgun and we found a gas can. I would whip it up in the air and Jim would shoot it with the first barrel, then it would start to come down and he'd shoot it again, causing it to go back up in the air. It was so cool. We were always dumping rocks down the ground hog holes.

Hockey on the pond was great. There was an assortment of equipment. I remember the skates always having dull blades and being four sizes too big for our feet. We were all skating more on our ankles than the blades. Somebody always managed to get a bloody nose. We were bundled up in 12 sheets of clothes that our parents wore when they were 12 years old. We looked like dirty Charley Browns out there. So even if we did fall down, we were well padded for protection.

I remember when Jim, Dave and I would swing out on the rope to drop in the pond. There were different kinds of swings:

- The swing out and just jump in
- The one where you climb up the tree and get on the far limb where you had a good trajectory to whip yourself out over the water
- The swing flip and dive and
- The swing followed by a one and one half.
- Sometimes, all three of us would get on the rope at the same time and do what we called the triple oscillator dive. We stood as far back as we could on the picnic table. We would determine ahead of time how many times we would swing back and forth before letting go. Finally we would all yell out "triple oscillator" and we'd try to dive in the water at the same time.

Basically the farm was an endless supply of absolute fun for every kid and it made me feel like someday I need to have a farm for my kids. It was so phenomenal to have all those things to do. Even if we couldn't think of things to do, we'd run to Grandma and ask, "Grandma what can we do"? She would always think of something like, "Go out in the chicken house and find something round, take it in the barn and kick it around." We all thought whatever she said was a wonderful idea. I will absolutely never forget that kind of fun on the farm.

Jenny Biller

Like my cousins, my memories of Grandma begin with the perception of a favored child. Not that Grandma had favorites, but that we were all made to feel like we were favorites. I was in the fourth grade before I realized that not all grandparents lived on a farm. I was far older when I realized that not everyone had such a wonderful grandmother.

Memories of Grandma are like a warm enveloping cloud. She provided a sense of caring stability. When you were with Grandma, all was well with the world. Her grandchildren were special in many ways that no other grandchild could hope to achieve. She was able to give each of us an added measure of confidence and self-worth. During summer visits she would always have some project that she would do just for me. Once she made a purse for me like the one we saw at Lazarus.

I never heard her say one negative word about any family member. She was always at our rescue. Once while cruising through West Milton, Mom was pulled over for speeding. Grandma insisted that Mom had done nothing wrong and if there was a fine she would pay it, always the protector.

As I ran into difficult challenges in life, Grandma was there. Her supportive words (mostly in letters) during times of personal illness or Dad's death will always remain in my memory. Grandma came to stay with Jimmy and I while Mom underwent diagnostic surgery for leukemia. I remember a sign we made for Mom when she came home. "Even though you've got no spleen, we think you're really keen."

Those of us with children of our own soon found that the supportive characteristics of our lineage were graciously passed on to our children. When we married the same was true of our spouses. The sheer nature of our selection indicated that the spouse must indeed be of fine quality. With Grandma it was always clearly understood that her family was the best the earth had to offer.

Grandma held herself to the highest standards and somehow managed to do so without being judgmental of others. It is rare to find someone so profusely good. Brad, Jimmy and I were playing nickel-dime poker at the farm and finally convinced Grandma to join. After explaining the rules to her, Grandma proceeded to whip us all. At the end of the game she fervently insisted upon giving us all the change back. "It's not right to gamble," she said quietly.

She taught us to enjoy life by sharing her love of life. We would take walks on the farm, stop to pick flowers and make hollyhock dolls, sit outside in the evening and enjoy the Midwest summer sunsets. I have not since found a sunset as beautiful as those that reside in my memory.

On a visit with Grandma a few years ago, I was thinking out loud, "I have never heard of or known anyone to be so loved and so adored by so many people."

"Still other seeds fell on good soil, where it produced a crop - a 100, 60 or 30 times what was sown" (Matthew 13:8). Grandma is the ultimate witness of how truly wealthy a person can become if they give from their heart. I look now to my own mother and see truly wonderful characteristics that were planted by Grandma. The number of patients touched by Mom's caring ways can no longer be counted. Looking for the good in everyone, truly trying to understand the person as well as the different perspectives and facing adversity in a positive way are traits which must have stemmed from Grandma. If I can plant even a small portion of those characteristics in my children, I will count myself lucky.

Jim S. Biller

I believe I can talk about this incident, now that the statute of limitations has run out. It seems that my Mom, Grandma and Grandpa were shopping, while Phil and I had the run of the whole farm. We were about 10 years old. First, we went to Grandpa's room. We were climbing up on top of things to see what we could find. Phil struck it rich! We found a propane torch with a nozzle. It didn't take much longer after that until we found a way to ignite it. We started lighting and burning stuff. We killed a few ants. Then we tried to burn a few trees, but couldn't ignite any. We learned later that sometimes a fire is out and sometimes a fire isn't really out. We were tooling around way out in the back. We had been lighting fires for probably 2 hours when Mom, Grandma and Grandpa came back and they wondered what all these little fires were doing all over the place. When they pulled up, they saw that the hickory stump on the far side of the garage was engulfed in flames. I am sure they were curious as to how that stump, along with many other objects caught fire. When they found us with the propane torch their questions were answered. We spent the next 2 hours carrying water to all the locations we had torched, fire or not. In those 2 hours we had probably watered down about 40 different things. After we finished that task, Grandpa had a little project for us, something to do with manure. I don't remember the details but I remember my Mom jumping on me and Phil's mom jumping on him, but I don't remember Grandma getting upset, she just let her daughters handle the situation.

Once, when I was 12 years old, Dave and I were playing in the barn. We thought we heard something, so we went back in the house. Grandma told us that maybe it was a rodent or some other animal. So we ran back out to check. But little did we know that Grandma was sneaking out behind us and she was the one making the noises. Pretty soon she just had us frantic running back and forth between the barn and the house. Finally we broke down and Grandma came back and told us that she was making the noises.

I remember the potions we used to make mostly with household products. Alcohol was especially fun because it would burn. It was always interesting to see what we could make, sometimes body excrements, or whatever. We would always try to get Jenny or Alison to drink them.

Ranya Studebaker

Grandma Studebaker will always be a mentor to me. She had a kind heart and she gave so much. I remember hearing about how forgiving Grandma was when Uncle Ted was killed. I always watch in awe when I see the video when Grandma and Grandpa were interviewed after Uncle Ted died. Being a mother, I always hope that I am as kind hearted but I honestly do not think that I would be that strong when my children are concerned. I fondly remember sitting beside Grandma while she talked about her parents, her-in laws, her children and grandchildren. We would often laugh or simply sigh throughout our conversations. In school, I would read about the Depression, but to hear it from Grandma, I felt my heart wrench for all the hungry and desperate people.

I can't believe there was actually a time when people would leave their doors unlocked and welcome unfortunate strangers into their home for a hot meal. We often think that we have it better than 60 or 70 years ago, but I doubt that we have the same trust in each other as Grandma's family had in people they did not even know. I always loved that Grandma would go to the trouble of making me and my siblings feel very loved. We were the youngest grandchildren for a long time and I felt a little left out when the older grandchildren would get together. But Grandma was always there to involve us in various activities like making paper flowers or playing outside. One Easter, Kendra and Chad had chicken pox while we were over at the farm for an Easter egg hunt. My mother and Grandma hid the eggs inside for Kendra and Chad so they would not feel sad. They also hid some eggs outside for us healthy ones.

When I was about 13 years old, Grandma had my name for Christmas. She had sewn a beautiful blue nightgown with a matching cover robe. Even when I grew out of it, I wouldn't part with it. Unfortunately, my gift burned in our house fire.

I remember staying over at the farm on weekends. That was always fun. Grandma would take us outside to pick grapes, many of which we would eat to our regret. One morning Grandma could not get us to eat our breakfast. She tried, giving us various dishes, but we were a stubborn bunch. All of a sudden Grandma's face lit up and she made ice cream cones and dipped them in cereal. What a smart Grandma! She would constantly come up with creative activities or ways to get us to eat our meals.

I was sad when Grandma and Grandpa went to Florida for the Winter. One Winter my family went down to visit which was fun. Grandma would always have food waiting for us, no matter whether she was home in Ohio or Florida. I liked listening to Grandma play the organ or watch her knit.

The highest compliment that Grandma ever gave me was when she said, "Ranya, you're a good mother." Coming from a mother that I could see no fault in was just pure gold. Grandma made Rich feel more than welcome when we became engaged and then a year later, married. Grandma was always so good at making people feel like part of the family, even if someone just joined after a few months. Rich and I only dated for just over a month before we became engaged. Unlike many people, Grandma did not think that things would not work out because she liked to have faith in everybody.

When Daniel was a baby, he spent a lot of time with Grandma. She lived with Ron and Evonne, my parents for about a year and a half. Many days I had to look for Daniel when he was crawling around and found him in Grandma's room. She wouldn't know that Daniel was in her room until she felt something nibbling on her toes. Since her eyesight was failing, this was her signal that Daniel was around. Sometimes he would climb on her bed and giggle. I really enjoyed watching my baby interact with Grandma. She seemed to have this certain touch with Daniel because I would take him to Grandma so she could rock him to sleep. Daniel would use her walker to learn to walk which tickled Grandma. I am so glad that she was able to spend time with Daniel. I know that Daniel was too young at the time to remember her but I'm so thankful that he spent time with her.

Ana wasn't able to spend time with Grandma like Daniel, because Grandma had moved to the Greenville nursing home. But I remember one visit which I have a picture to look back on. Aunt Linda was in the room when Rich, Daniel, Ana and I arrived. Linda was brushing Grandma's hair, which comforted both of them. Ana seemed fascinated with all of Grandma's white hair so she grabbed a handful, I was horrified that Grandma was hurt; but Grandma thought that it was Aunt Linda still brushing and liked the pull. During that visit, Ana and Daniel would take turns going into the hall to entertain some of the residents. I'm so glad we visited that day. I felt heartbroken because Grandma seemed to be in a different time or place during that visit. I was thankful that at that time Grandma's eye sight was gone, so she wouldn't see tears flow down my face as we talked. Although I could keep my voice strong, I couldn't stop the tears. In my heart, I knew this was going to be the last time I would see my mentor who taught me so much and loved me so much. I was right because Grandma passed away less than a month later. Grandma, you are still teaching me to be a good person and mother. You sacrificed so much to stay home with your children. I hope that I can follow your footsteps with my own children. I love you and miss you.

Tarik Studebaker

These are some of my fondest memories of Grandma Studebaker. Probably the strongest memory is that she always had an ample supply of Archway Cookies on hand for anyone who cared to have one. She would always offer one to me as a snack or dessert after lunch. The ones with jelly centers were the best. Grandma definitely knew the way to my heart. During the summer time, she was always sending us out to the barn or pond to play. I always thought she was just getting us involved with the outside. Now I know that she just wanted to get a break from the throngs of children running around the house getting into all the things we should not be getting into.

Kendra Sherman

Thinking of Grandma makes me remember many wonderful days at the farm. I remember playing hide and seek in the barn with Ranya, Tarik and Chad and of course jumping off the rope and swimming in the pond. As a child, I remember Grandma had a terrific imagination. She somehow found a way to keep the attention of all four of us kids, so we never felt bored. One particular evening, Ranya and I sat with Grandma in the family room on the davenport. Grandma had set out lots of construction, paper, scissors and glue. She showed Ranya and I how to make construction paper tulips and other flowers. I think the three of us must have made different kinds of flowers for what seemed like hours. It was wonderful.

Grandma would buy some of our favorite foods. Before we would come and stay for a weekend at the farm. She always had Captain Crunch or something else for us for breakfast and I remember thinking that was so special because we weren't allowed to have "sugar cereals" at home. Of course, every grandchild remembers the cookies Grandma always had in the bread box!

At the farm, I remember swinging on the willow tree branches across the Creek. Grandma and Grandpa would sit on the porch rockers and watch us as we played in the swing or out in the yard.

Grandma always inspired me. She is someone I truly adore and have always looked up to. When I was in college I took a women's studies class and one of my assignments was to interview and write a paper about a woman who was born before 1925. I chose to write about Grandma's life so I called her and interviewed her over the telephone since I was in California and she was in Ohio. During my several interviews with her, I came to see Grandma in a different light. I learned so much about her as a woman, not just my Grandma. When I finished the paper, I sent a copy to Grandma. Less than one week later, I got a beautiful card in the mail from her with a 20 dollar check! I couldn't believe Grandma actually paid me for doing my college homework. It was really a wonderful experience for me to learn so much about a woman I admire and love.

Grandma was one of the very best letter writers! She really spent a lot of time thinking about words to capture your attention. She always knew just the perfect thing to say in her letters or cards to make you feel so loved and think that somehow everything would work out all right. I have many unforgettable memories about Grandma when she lived with my parents, Ron and Evonne. One day I ripped a pair of shorts that I really liked and Grandma said she would mend them for me. Her eyes began to get worse during this time but she was so insistent to do my shorts anyway. She spent a long time fixing them so they were just perfect. It wasn't until later that I realized the shorts had a little blood on them where Grandma had poked her fingers with the needle when she was fixing them. I cried when I saw that because I realized what a labor of love it was for Grandma to fix the shorts for me.

Some nights, Brent and I would go to Grandma's room and sit and talk to her about all kinds of things. Grandma would talk to Brent about what it was like when she was a teacher and the two of them would compare "teacher stories." A few times Grandma referred to Brent as Bruce and Brent and I would look at each other and smile and never say anything. Grandma had a wonderful way of telling stories where Brent and I would just want to sit and listen to her talk for hours. She told us what it was like in the early years of marriage to Grandpa and what it was like with all the kids on the farm.

When her health began to get worse, I never heard Grandma complain. Her spirit was always strong and her mood was always bright and cheery even if her body was failing her. Despite everything that was going on, she always found a way to put her troubles aside and make everyone around her feel better.

I really miss Grandma today. We have an angel on our mantle that Grandma gave us a long time ago, and when we look at it, we feel as if she is still around us. The more I reflect on her, the more I realize the profound impact she has had on my life. I wish she was still here so I could talk to her some more and get her advice about things. The more I talked to Grandma the better I felt about things and the more I learned about life in general. She was the best Grandma anyone could ever ask for.

Chad Studebaker

To Grandma,

Oh, my dear Grandmother, oh how I miss thee! I think of you often, sometimes sad and others glad! Sometimes in the morning, sometimes in the middle of the day and sometimes in the kitchen, just one of your favorite places, others just outside hanging clothes on the line in the orchard. Sometimes I found you on the porch or in the family room, the fan going, screen door open and the wind whistling through while you read a good book. Often I saw you with a pencil and paper to express yourself to those farther away. You always had time for a question or a discussion to those curious minds around you like mine. You had a persona about yourself like no other, I have known, one that gave and gave of yourself until everyone was more than satisfied. As I now realize you set the precedent like no other in everything you did or said. You always worked harder than anyone else, always worked before everyone else, read, more than anyone, wrote more letters than anyone, cared more than others, gave more than others and definitely cooked more than anyone else. You always set a pace to be achieved. The example you set for those to follow and all the things you taught along the way, mean so much.

Grandmother, I cannot express to you in words what your life meant to me. I reflect often on the memories I have shared with you. Spending the first week after school at the farm, sometimes even two weeks, I would rummage through all the old books, photos, Grandpa's office and little gadgets, went fishing, helped Dwaine (farmer and family friend) replant the crop along the driveway. I also helped him with mowing and repairs along the creek to maintain a good water flow.

Oh, the fond memories that will last forever. I often enjoyed just reading or sitting in the living room with windows open and feeling the breeze as we would discuss life, the world and our aspirations for the future. You always have the best questions to stimulate the conversation or to find out what I thought! We always had so much in common, including our interests in the future! I love just finding out what the past was like. I would ask you about the Great Depression, WWII, my dad and growing up in the early 1900s! The conversations intrigued me so. I could always see the past very clearly through your eyes as if I had seen it myself. All your wisdom and words of advice were always there at the right time and were ever so helpful. If I could only take you with me in my pocket for a rest of my life, but I know that you are with me wherever I go, however it is sometimes not the same.

With all my love,
Chad Richard Studebaker

Ramona Studebaker

I am so thankful that Grandma sent Amelia Badilla books to me in California. She knew I liked funny stories. When she visited us, she read stories to me. She also made animal sounds and played songs for us on the piano. I liked visiting Grandma and Grandpa in Ohio. She had games for me to play and things for me to do in activity books.

Mackenzie Studebaker

I remember Grandma visiting me when I was very young and reading stories and singing songs to me. She wrote a lot to us and we would call her and thank her for the letters and have nice talks. When she was at Greenville and couldn't see well, I would put my hand on her and say, "This is Mackenzie." She would smile because she was just a nice lady. From what I know about Zelma, if any of her children happened to do anything wrong, there was a circle on the ground that they would have to put their nose in. When my Mom heard that, she started doing that to us.

I remember when I was playing with my tea party set, Grandma played with me. At the end I was so tired I could hardly pick up anything so she did a favor for me and picked up everything and I gave her a kiss. If she would have been my teacher, I would have been comfortable with her because I know she was a good teacher. If I were to entitle a book about her, I would probably call it, "Memories of a Very Good Friend" or "Flip Flops Down Main Street." My dad told me that's what she said she would do when she got to heaven.

Chapter 5

Photographs

"Family is what grounds you."
Angelina Jolie

Coelestine and Elnora Leiber (Zelma's maternal grandparents)

Fred and Elnora (Zelma's parents with Mary Ann)

Zelma, Coelestine (Zelma's Grandfather), Emerson

Zelma

Emerson, Zelma

Siblings: Loyal, Pauline, Emerson, Zelma

Zelma 1925

Zelma, high school graduation

Zelma, first year teacher

Wedding day June 14, 1929, Mennonite Church, Englewood, OH

Front: Marjorie Roth Stemple, Back Row: Dale Studebaker, Mary Katherine Studebaker Beachler, Stanley and Zelma Studebaker, Lois Neher, Paul Studebaker

Home where Zelma grew up, Englewood, OH

Zelma and Mary Ann, Route 48 Union, OH

Marysville, OH home

Stanley and Zelma with Mary Ann, Nancy, Linda and Lowell at home on Route 48

Left to right: Mary Ann, Gary, Nancy, Linda, Lowell, Ron at Route 55 west of Troy, OH

County Line Farm, Union, OH 1946 - 1996

Seated: Gary, Lowell, Zelma, Doug, Stanley, Mary Ann, Ted
Standing: Nancy, Ron, Linda

Stanley and Zelma in the early 1950s

Zelma at the County Line Farm

Doug and Zelma peeling apples at the church

Zelma and Doug beside Stanley's Vagabond Airplane

Zelma, Elementary Teacher, May 1963

Zelma and Stanley 1964

Verda Mae Peters and Zelma at the
March on Washington, August 1963

Zelma and Stanly at Miami University
graduation, August, 1968

Stanley and Zelma at Church Conference

Pakdy and Zelma

Books celebrating Ted's life

Zelma meets her cousin, Genoviva Dorflinger in
Niedereschach, Germany, 1975

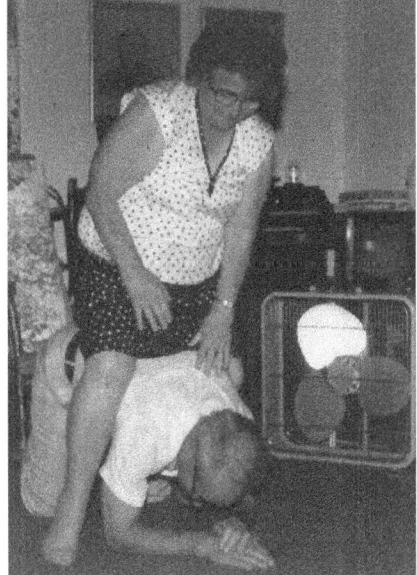

Wrestling fun with Stanley

Enjoying the organ

At an ocean beach in Florida

50th wedding anniversary celebration

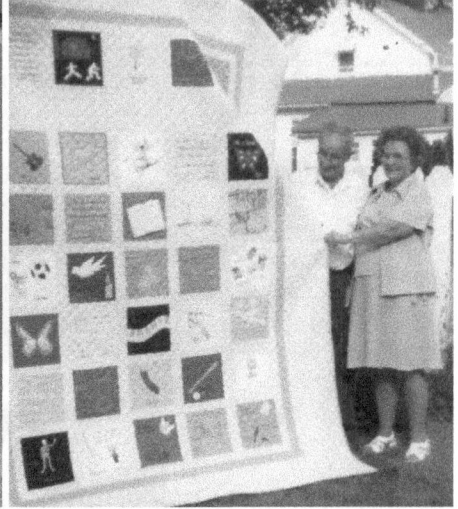
50th wedding anniversary quilt

First row: Nancy, Zelma, Stanley   Second row: Susan, Gary, Evonne, Linda, Jim
Third row: Mary Ann, Milton   Fourth row: Ron, Doug, Lowell

Sebring, Florida

Lake Placid, Florida home

A view from the Lake Placid Tower

Retirement years

Reading to Ramona

Fun with Mackenzie

Diary writing

Extended family at Brethren Retirement Community, Christmas 1993

Three generations return to the farm to remember the great times, August, 1994

Brethren Retirement Community
Christmas 1993

Brethren Retirement Community

Zelma at Ron and Evonne's farm

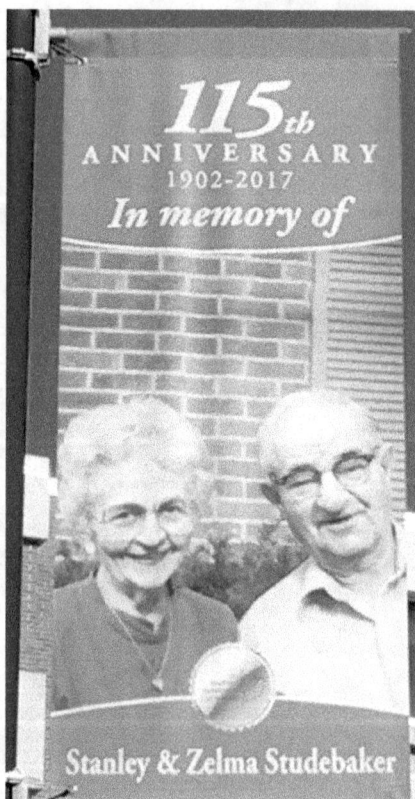

Banner at the
Brethren Retirement Community

Chapter 6

Poetry and Short Stories

"There are just so many stories that are buried on family trees."
Henry Louis Gates

Zelma found that written communication gave her the pleasure of creative expression. Wordsmithing came natural and she was attracted to the challenge of finding the right words or phrases for the occasion, accordingly she was adept at word games. She attended a creative writing seminar in Wisconsin and took pride in developing her writing skills during her studies at Miami University.

Her creative side was evident in her poetry and short stories. She delighted in developing her topics with descriptors that brought her stories to life. She saw the need for people to fulfill personal hopes and dreams and to be bolstered along the way. Writing was a natural way for her to connect with loved ones to accomplish her communicative desires. She enjoyed finding choice words to express herself. Therefore, she kept a Thesaurus and other writing manuals available. Her letters were sometimes known for being detailed and lengthy.

Zelma occasionally enclosed a poem with a Christmas gift or for family celebrations. Some of her children asked her to write a poem for them to be included with a gift to a friend. She obliged with an on the spot poem to fit the occasion. Zelma's children and some of her grandchildren have also written poetry or greetings for family celebrations. Each composition contributed to the fun at these gatherings.

Included here are some of her many poems she wrote for her immediate family, grandchildren, great grandchildren and friends. The last part of this chapter includes selections from her short stories.

Poetry

Stanley

This is our Grandfather there is no doubt
That he started the family this story's about.

In other words as you'll plainly see
He is the root of our family tree.

He learned from his forebears, all men of the soil
That life's richest blessings reward humble toil.

Now when in manhood a true Studebaker,
He courted a girl and decided to take 'er.

Said he, "As a wife she'll just fit the bill!"
His choice was a wise one cause he's got 'er still.

And so all the branches and twigs on the tree,
Grew from Grandfather's venture in matrimony.

Our Daddy's bunch grew with vigor and vim.
It takes lots of pages to tell about him.

Though smallest of stature and not very big,
His prolific limb produced tag after twig.

Lots of deep "laugh" lines are traced on his face;
When he turns on his smile, it lights up the place.

For years they have plowed and planted their acres,
But the best crop of all is there eight Studebakers.

And though complications arise frequently,
Life never gets dull in this family.

Mary Ann
The Advent of our First Born

Incredible incidents… awesome indeed,
Are everyday fair in our clan,
But none can surpass for ecstatic delight,
The night that we got Mary Ann!

We'd been to a concert and Grandma's house too.
Then home and in bed by eleven.
A short few hours later that long legged-bird
Delivered our bundle from heaven!

Two whole weeks early! What a surprise!
Doctor G. lived just a short distance,
But would this kid await his arrival? Oh, no!
She'd manage without his assistance.

With a mind of her own, stark naked she came
Wearing only her wee self-esteem.
A faint hint of smile on her rosebud mouth
And prone to get on with her dream.

The very first grandchild on our family tree!
The news spread fast that morn.
Relatives all poured in to admire
The most beautiful babe ever born.

How perfect and cuddly! What soft, tiny feet!
Comments rolled off every tongue;
But old Johnny Stump's profound observation
Was simply, "My ain't she young?"

And forever young as she strides through the days
Shadows and sun interlace;
To endow her with wisdom, laughter and love,
But caring is her special grace!

Fifty six years have endeared her to us
And pride constrains me to add:
Beyond all doubt she's the most perfect first-born
Her dad and I ever had!
October 3, 1986.
Mary Ann's 56th birthday.

Lowell

Granddaughters are nice, but when all's said and done,
No family's complete without a grandson.

Now we aim to please so to everyone's joy,
One August morning, we welcomed a boy.

Things got more lively with Lowell's arrival.
"Always on guard" seemed our rule for survival!

Eventually harnessed, this "go power" and "steam,"
Won him a place on the varsity team.

And helped him at the state fair, when he was sixteen,
To win first place with his Guernsey, Irene.

Though football and farming rate top notch with Bub,
He's happiest when flying the old Piper Cub.

Nancy

This next little twig brought our account up to three,
A dear little girl whom we named Nancy Lee.

Her sweet disposition and good nature too,
Made us all think. "She's too good to be true!"

Besides being good, she's alert and ambitious.
Her cookies, cakes and pies are delicious.

She makes jam and jelly, she can process and freeze.
Any food we produce from poultry to peas.

She loves to sew and make all of her clothes,
But what she is thinking, nobody knows.

Linda

Next after Nancy comes Linda Louise.
Some folks believe they're alike as two peas.

While identification is not always simple,
She's always best known as the one with the dimple.

She loves a good time, and as everyone knows,
She always has fun wherever she goes.

She's a lover of sports, any kind you can name.
Her greatest delight is in playing the game.

Ron

The day dawned crisp and sunny in October '37.
We've been eagerly expecting one more bundle from heaven.

Mom was as pregnant as it's possible to get.
My answer to Grandma was, "No Mom, Nothing yet."

So excitement ran at high pitch on our Marysville farm,
When suddenly Mom sounded her familiar alarm.

All had gone well and the doc left the scene
The family rushed in to welcome Ronald Dean!

Everyone held the new little guy
With a dimple and mischief in his eye.

Years ago this cuddly charmer
Has been social worker, flyer and farmer.

As a teenage driver, he had a few tricks,
Scaring chickens off the road, he got his kicks.

Let adventure beckon and Ron followed on the double.
His instinct and daring got him in trouble.

Saved by an angel, on a wing and a prayer,
Cause the dimple's still intact and he still has some hair.

So blessings on you Ron and birthday love galore!
Here's to a happy fortieth and many, many more!

October 6, 1977
Ron's fortieth birthday

89

Gary

Our calendar's circled date February 9th,
A most auspicious date.
A family highlight so superb,
We've got to celebrate.

We'd lived three years on our Marysville farm,
Raising dairy cows, grain and hay.
Now our farm sale was scheduled in less than 2 weeks
And we were moving away.

Mary Ann was nine and Lowell seven.
Nancy was just a half dozen.
Linda and Ronnie were four and two
and now our household is buzzin'!

The new model Studie was on the way,
And we thought it would be fittin' and proper
To even things out so - we eagerly hoped,
That there was a boy in the hopper

Grandma and Grandpa had just arrived
To visit a day or two,
And we all started supper when the moment of truth
Struck like a bolt from the blue.

The signal was sharp, unmistakably clear;
We'd soon be joined by another.
And two hours later our whole family circle,
Was admiring our new baby brother!

A plump blue eyed boy, "Eight pounds," Dr. said,
Blond ringlets of hair softly curled.
There was never a doubt from his moment of birth,
This child would bless the world.

And so it has been in those forty short years
Our predictions all have come true,
But our entire family proclaims his best gift
Ramona Linda and Sue.

Ted

He talked of many things but made it clear
He had decided his life would be directed
To some type of social work and he would
Probably be gone from home for good.

If Ted had known this was to happen,
I am sure he would have gone right ahead.
In one way, his death is an even greater witness
Then had he lived.

With the sure knowledge that like the metamorphosis
That butterfly had passed through and shedding its cocoon
And emerging a gorgeous butterfly to sore wherever it
chooses, just so, Ted now shed his mortal body and his
Spirit would now allow him to witness unhindered in
Many more places than before.

Doug

Goodbye all said, I waved him out of sight,
I turn to find the old familiar ache
Still there. The fledgling, eager poised for flight,
Departing leaves a vacuum in its wake.

A rush of deafen silence strikes my ears,
To rise like sudden wind before a rain,
The force made more intense by all the years
When noise and laughter on this house have lain.

Like rolling fog and wisps of memory curl,
Within me grateful prayers begin to rise.
I tell his dad, "We'd better warn the world
He's going to try it on for size!"

And once again, in poignant interlude,
I laugh and learn the grace of gratitude.

Pakdy

I think it's such a lovely thing
To plant a garden in the spring.
Some nice straight rows I measure there
And sow the seeds with tender care.

Then God sends rain and sunshine bright
And soon my garden's a wondrous sight.
I pick golden carrots and red tomatoes,
Purple turnips and white potatoes.

Cabbages, lettuce and beans,
Spinach and all the salad greens,
My corn and squash are yellow,
Don't you think I'm a lucky fellow?
November 15, 1977

Julia

This enormous teddy bear
Is enamored of your charms!
You'll always get a bear hug
When you cuddle in his arms!

Craig and Cindy

If your puzzled 'bout pruning or spraying,
Or mulching, or working your ground,
This is a stand in for Brian,
In case he isn't around.

Jill

Store your family memories here;
Be sure to fill every page.
You realize 50 years from now
It's your passport to happy old age!

Diane

Fill this with snapshots
Then when your old;
With your grandchildren milling about,
You'll discover that you've got clout!

Brian

You'll soon be a wealthy nurseryman,
Prime target for assault by some crank,
So we got you a bullet proof suitcase
To carry your cash to the bank.

Brad

A band director you may be
Or some kind of musical big cheese.
But your Gramps from his vast experience insists,
"Dadburn! You can't live without these!"

Dan

If dawn finds you somnolent, recumbent, inert,
Helplessly prone and supine,
This timely device routs lethargy fast,
And compels you to rise and shine.

Amy

This gift won't keep the frigid breeze
Off your lovely feet or face,
But it might protect the bony shell
That holds your brain in place.

Dave

A surgeon with scalpel can mend your crushed bones,
But if you should crunch up your car,
Just take it to Dave, your body shop man,
The surgeon with a mean wrecking bar.

Philip
Recommendation for a High Class Attorney

Sure as butter is churn-y
So his mind has been learn-y
And I'll be gol-durn-y
If you'll find a keener attorney
Herewith
Than Philip Smith.

Ranya

The Florida stores had hearts for girls,
Red and yellow and blue,
But we chose these pink ones right away,
Because they remind us of you!

Tarik

There's something you love that "sticks to your ribs."
Its peanut butter and jelly!
This gift not only sticks to your ribs,
But also to your back and belly!

Kendra

This "rosy" gift seemed exactly right,
It's elegant and precise.
Shouting our sentiments to the world:
"We think you're pretty nice!"

Chad

Want to act out a riddle? Just put on this gift.
Start whirling! And don't you dare stop!
Now what are you doing? Can anyone guess?
Why you're actually spinning your top!

Aaron

We'll give you a tune up and a good lube job
Before you start on vacation.
We'll check your tires and fill up your tank
At Aaron's service station!

Zachary

Have your Toyota serviced at Zach's,
He'll fix you up fine and dandy.
You'll like doing business, No need for cash.
He'll accept payment in candy.

Joshua

This whistling locomotive
Zooms down the track.
Just be very careful
So you don't run into Zach!

Christmas Eve

It's Christmas Eve, the snowflakes flutter down.
They gently glide like birds of purest white
In their slow way through the Holy Night,
Spreading a feathery blanket on the ground,

Winging to earth without a sound.
Then in the darkened sky appears a light,
The sleigh with Santa on his annual flight.
For boys and girls the moment is profound.

The magic joys of Christmas fill their dreams.
The house is filled with happiness and mirth.
If we could learn to share all this joyous good,
The world would be a better place it seems.

And peace would be reality on earth,
And men could come to know true brotherhood.

A Mother's Day Prayer.

Thank thee God for Mother Dear.
Her sweet smile brings heaven near.
For her love so like thine own
That to me thy love has shown.

By her sacrifice to me
I can now more clearly see
In thy tender loving face
All the mercies of thy grace.

Thank thee for thy gift so rare.
Thank thee God for mother's care.
Father hear me as I pray
In my simple childlike way.

Guard and love and keep her
Ever in Thy favor.
Let the things I say and do
Honor thee and mother too.

Let thine angels hover
Keeping watch above her.
Bless her tenderly today
This in Jesus name I pray.

Written for the Troy Church of the Brethren.
Junior Choir, April 1958

To Eva Lightner, (Treasurer for women's work)

This little card bears sad information.
Our treasury's suffering from deflation.
Though usually plump,
The old summer slump
Has invaded its bloodstream and set up stagnation.

Our outreach is hampered; No funds if you please,
To help the needy or give Kingdom keys.
Now prescribed correction
Is immediate injection
Of a little fresh cash to arrest the disease.

We searched for a way to replenish the till
Where effort required is practically nil.
We reached the conclusion
That for least confusion
A Foodless Bake Sale would just fill the bill.

No food to donate, nothing to buy.
These simple instructions will help you comply.
Just figure the cost
Plus time you'd have lost
To bake and deliver the sweets.

Then send the amount which you think you should
By the end of the week or as soon as you could.
And quick as a wink we'll be in the pink.
Our thanks to you, may the Lord bless you good.
August 1959

To the Young Marrieds' Class

It's a carry in meal; There's fun in the air.
It's a birthday party and we want you there.

On Sunday, March 5, 5 o'clock on the dot.
Each month has a table; you find your spot.

You'll be entertained while, your "fined" and dined.
Yes, wait till you see what we have in mind.

"Fined" did we say? Well here are the facts.
Uncle Sam levies his income tax,

But we've a more painless way to dig gold.
We'll penalize you for growing old.

The amount of your fine is easy to gauge,
Just dole out a dime for each year of your age.

Now remember the date and come we insist.
Our pledge will be met and this case dismissed.
March 1961

Old Mother Hubbard

Nursery rhymes hold nuggets of truth
So says pastor Bob, Forsooth, Forsooth.

Consider the motives of dear sister Hubbard,
Despite the deplorable state of her cupboard.

She devoutly believed what the good book said,
That we fellowship truly in the breaking of bread.

But her efforts were thwarted…not a crumb was in sight.
Now we find ourselves in a difficult plight.

We have our new church but our kitchen is bare,
There isn't a cupboard, nor food items there.

Since eating together helps nourish the soul,
To dispense hospitality must be our role.

So without more ado or more of this verse,
Let every good sister dig down in her purse.

And send in a gift with love and a prayer.
God bless our kitchen as together, we share.
June 1961

97

To Fred Rice, Prospective Father
(Written for Stanley to advise Fred)

Take it from me, a tired father of eight,
There are a few facts I'm constrained to relate.

Though you are now filled with joy and elation,
There will be times when you'll need some sedation.

Though aspirin helps, you must face the facts,
There are very few times when Pop can relax.

When baby wails loudly and there's no relief,
There's nothing so useful as a big handkerchief.

It mops your tired brow or wipes tiny nose.
When formula spills, it cleans off your clothes.

You've donned you're white shirt, but baby spills juice,
Just motion to Dottie and signal a truce.

You can stuff nursery keyhole to muffle the wails.
You can wipe drooling mouth and if all this fails,

It's a time-honored gadget to play peek-a-boo,
So luck to you Fred and "Frederica" too.

(Given with aspirin and white handkerchiefs)
March 1958

To Howard and Anna Dohner

A rainbow span of 50 years,
You've walked through pain and pleasure.
And true to legend rainbows yield
Rich rewards of treasure.

The Peace of God within your hearts,
The friends you have and hold,
Family ties knit strong with love,
These are your pot of gold.
September 1969

To Inez Lowry My Teacher Friend

Oh Inez was a friend of mine
In the good ole days of yore.
We taught school in old Shank Hall
Where we found fun galore.

She wore a smile 'bout ten yards wide,
Her laugh was sure contagious,
And yet the tricks she played on me
Were just downright outrageous.

She gave to me a box of candy.
It looked so delicious and pure,
But do you know what it turned out to be?
Just balls of old horse manure.

So watch for this gal and her tricks.
As a friend, she's fine and dandy,
But proceed with caution if she gives you a box
Of her famous Road Apple Candy.

To the Valley Forge Staff
(the school where Zelma taught)

Its people like you.
With your wonderful ways
Who've added such joy
To my Valley Forge days.

And in all my tomorrows
Wherever I go,
You'll inhabit my thoughts
And set them all aglow.
June 2, 1977

To Betty Sotzing
(A Brethren Volunteer Service worker)

If I could have just one wish
That really would come true,
Do you know what I'd wish for
And what I'd like to do?

I'd like to drop in on you,
And chat a little while
And wish you "Merry Christmas"
In good old fashion style.

A greeting card is lovely
With pictures to enhance it,
And the wish expressed is warm
But it cools off so in transit.

So I'll just make my own wish
To lite you like a glove.
I'll take it from my heart
And I wrap it up with love.

I'll insulate it all around
With warmest thoughts of cheer,
And may it set your heart a glow
Throughout the coming year.

And then I'll tie and label it,
"Especially for Betty,"
And may heaven's choicest blessings
Shower you like confetti.
December 1950

Good Wishes Garden Variety

So you had an operation!
Well I want you to know,
It BEETS me when I think of it,
'Cos you BEAN fillin' low.

An' Harvey can't do nothin' much
"Cept just sit an' pine
When his rosy cheeked TOMATO
Is droopin' on the vine.

Makes a MANGO home at night
Feelin' mighty sad,
When doctors start a carvin' up
The only wife he had.

So LETTUCE hear you're better soon,
Feeling fine and fit,
An' when good health returns to you
Jus' CABBAGE onto it.

PEAS TURNIP soon at home again
If you really CARROT all,
Where nurses won't be GARDEN you
And I can come to call.

The Bard of the Bean Patch.
April 1975

To Perry and Lauree Huffaker

It took some observation
And some conjugation too,
To determine something proper
For our Christmas gift to you.

There was much to be considered
For the gift we had in mind.
Must be glamorous yet useful
When your guests are wined and dined.

Now it comes to our attention
(Quite by chance, you understand),
The old parsonage bread box
Was held shut by rubber band.

Now rubber bands are useful.
They once were all the rage,
But magnetic closures are the thing
In this modern day and age.

When parishioners come calling,
And are glancing round your home,
They can wow their friends by boasting
Their bread box is of chrome.

We racked our brains still further
And we had another hunch,
We thought you'd like to glamorize
The serving of your punch.

It's nice to serve by pitcher
When you pour for any guest
But dipping from a punch bowl
Will leave them more impressed.

Our humble Brethren background
Was part of our design,
To help when you're dispensing
The parsonage bread and wine.

To Margaret Harshbarger

So you've had a "LITTLE LUMP" removed.
What a subtle way to tell it.
Well I've had eight of them removed
But I was one to YELL it.

Of course the styles were different then,
No SHIFTS to hide the bump,
No chic HAIRDOS of gorgeous JEWELS (ahem)
To draw attention to your Lump.

But now your little secret's out
And this is to convey,
Our congratulations
And HAPPY MOTHER'S DAY!
May 1964

The End of Shank Hall Fatso Club

The pressure is off for all former fatties
We melted down pounds of that lard.
But be not deceived - those inches return
The minute you let down your guard.

Your best friends won't tell you you're putting on weight
But this little tape tells no lies.
So use it and follow its candid advice
For a neat little tummy and thighs.

To Margaret Fessler

I marvel how you deal with pain
With ample reason to complain.

You try instead to find a way
To brighten someone else's day.

You could resent those morning soaks
But that's the time you cheer up folks.

You're busy pen begins to fly
Across the pages till by and by

You're chatty notes endow and bless
A person's day with happiness.

And you instead of gripes and groans
Turn stumbling blocks to stepping stones.
April 1990

Short Stories

Self Portrait

Whatever I am, I must be a part of all that has touched me. At least I don't like to feel entirely responsible for my foibles. So perhaps if I dig around in the accumulation of biological facts and experiences that make up my background, I may be able to unearth some evidence that there is an explanation for me.

Perhaps the most fortunate of my early achieves, though I had nothing to do with it, was to become a member of a family in which we were taught that daily doses of work, play and relaxation, generously sprinkled with lots of fun and sharing, was a pretty good formula for a well-balanced life. We were blessed with wonderful parents of German ancestry whose ideas about thrift, honest toil and belief in God were so thoroughly etched in our minds that they have become an integral part of our make-up. By the same token, their firm conviction about such matters as deceit, laziness, cheating and gossip were also etched not infrequently with a hairbrush upon another part of our anatomies with long lasting results.

In all probability the best gifts they gave me were fortitude and a sense of humor, both of which are pretty vital equipment for a mother of eight. They have helped me ride out many a storm.

By nature I am more timid than daring. Many times I hesitate at the very threshold of what I want so much to do, fearful that I can't do it. Then comes along a spark of pluck and fortitude which sets off a charge that shoves me right through, and away I go, bubbling with enthusiasm for whatever is going to happen next. And it will happen, never fear. All I need to do is cup my hands and it is sure to rain either adventure or a terrible dilemma. So win or lose, I always get a bonus pay-off, either through the humor or the tragedy of it.

I wish I were not so obstinate about changing my mind. I am slow to come to a definite opinion and reluctant to give it up without plenty of sound reasons. I am prone to get involved in too many things with too little time to accomplish anything. Nevertheless, I manage to survive hectic days without too much wear and tear, probably because it seems less exhausting to cope with things calmly. I am not easily upset and it takes quite a lot of pressure to rouse my temper, but once it is roused I have a real battle to hold it down.

I find relaxation in many small things: sewing, letter writing, church work, music and walking in the rain, but mostly I love people. I am especially drawn to those under 3 months and over eighty years. Both seem to possess a delicate, ethereal quality that denotes a close proximity to heaven. But my one great obsession is babies and small children. Nothing so envelopes me in such a rosy cloud of contentment as to be surrounded by them and the more the merrier. I feel a kindred spirit to every hen clucking to her brood and to every Robin chirping to her perpetually hungry young. My greatest literary fault is evident - I am too wordy.
February 15, 1958

Hobo Christmas

It was early Christmas morning and the three little Studebakers were up long before their usual time. Gifts had been opened the night before and we were going to Grandpa and Grandma Roth's for the big family Christmas dinner and another gift exchange around their tree. The big Depression of the 30s was still hanging over us like an ominous presence, so our gifts to each other as well as other family members, had to be homemade articles from towels and clothing to hand-contrived games, doll clothes and food. During the night it had begun to snow and the prospect of a white Christmas made it perfect. Mary Ann and Lowell played with their gifts from Christmas Eve and I bathed Nancy and gave her breakfast as we waited for dad to finish milking and the barn work.

Suddenly it began to snow so hard we could hardly see the barn about 50 yards north of our house along the highway. The already strong wind took on gale proportions. Snow piled up and drifted rapidly. Traffic on Route 48 had slowed to a creep and moved with difficulty in the face of screaming wind and blinding snow. Then Grandma called and advised us to stay home; my sister and two brothers could not make it and the storm was getting worse. Some power lines were down so I got some of our canned beef and broth and made a huge pot of vegetable soup. It would be so good to stay in our warm house with hot soup and enjoy the day with family, games and radio.

Dad was late coming from the barn but that was understandable with extra hay and grain to prepare and warm bedding to spread for the twenty or more cows in the face of the blizzard.

Suddenly we thought we saw a lone figure walking or trying desperately to walk down the highway. As he made slow stumbling progress, we saw that it was apparently an old man in a long black tattered overcoat, an old cap pulled down over his ears and some old rags wrapped over his face with only a slit for his eyes. The wind raged and the snow was so deep now that he fought with every step to stay on the highway. I knew immediately that it was another poor homeless character, one of many who during these hard times, walked the highways asking for a bit of food and sometimes offered to do some small job for a meal.

I was so glad the soup was ready. I gathered the three children and told them this hobo would surely stop at our house and it was going to be a wonderful Christmas after all, because they were going to help me fix a good dinner for this poor, half frozen, hungry man who had no home to go to. They set out soup bowls and crackers and brought up canned peaches, pickles and etc.

They watched as the wind whipped his long coat around and sure enough, he was turning into our driveway. They followed me to the door and we opened it before he had time to knock, telling him to come in and get warm.

Just inside he stomped the snow on the old mat and pulled the snowy rags off his face saying, "Get this coat off and get me something hot to eat. We're not leaving this house today!" It was Dad who had found the old coat hanging in the barn. He'd walked the highway because the drifts between the house and the barn were too deep. No hobo, but we fed him anyway and had a great Christmas and went to Grandma's much later.

Trouble Is an Asset

Strange indeed, are the various attitudes with which people view difficulties and obstacles. To some, difficulties are things to be avoided at all costs. If perhaps, fate decrees that they shall be met, then the world owes those brave souls who suffer for all their worth, sympathy, pity, feathers in their cap or any of the various soothing syrups by which men sugar coat or coddle their egos. Still others, when the going gets tough, look for the easy way out at all costs.

It is these costs that concern me, because there is value lost whenever we meet a situation with less than our best, just as there are rich rewards for all who face life with courage and purpose. The degree of boldness to face the challenges and learn from them, will determine the measure of happiness and satisfaction we derive from them.

To each of us is given the gift of life to be lived. The gift, when first received, is made of pliable stuff. It is ours to shape and mold. To each is also given the tools for shaping and molding the mind with its miraculous reasoning power and the will by which we may translate thinking into intelligent action. The tools are in our hands, the life is before us and the decision is ours as to how we use the tools and what shall be the form and nature of the design which we create.

Shall we fashion merely a beautiful ornament, rigid and immobile, to be admired and enjoyed but useless? Or shall it have both beauty and usefulness, designed with flexibility for action, progress and for service? How shall we equip our lives? With good sturdy walking shoes for climbing the heights of discovery and adventure, or with a large size hitchhikers thumb so that we may flag down the more ambitious travelers and ride along on their steam?

Shall we be content with the valley view, or are we willing to find a way to climb higher for the more encompassing view from the mountain top? If the goal is the heights, then thank God for difficulties. For how shall we make progress in a perpendicular direction over a smooth surface?

Troubles are the sharp projecting crags by which we must lift ourselves. Every crag attained rewards us with a slightly broader view. Looking back, we can better understand the road we've traveled. Our experiences become more meaningful and we treasure them for their richness, depth and color. The business of living becomes a fascinating thing, exhilarating and inspiring. And with every obstacle successfully met and conquered, comes a strangely unique sense of satisfaction and happiness.

Slaying the dragons is not accomplished without courage, an overwhelming determination and hard work. Casper Milquetoast and his vacillating friends have not a single dragon head to display in their trophy cases. Such heads come too high for them and for the rigid, tense souls who panic, then resist and break, rather than learn the discipline of bending with the blows of fate.

Only the truly courageous and daring may achieve. For without the willingness to face trouble and to cope with it intelligently with the best that is within us, the joy is lost and hence the reward. For the sheer joy of it is our priceless reward.

And finally we must learn how to keep that joy for if we try to hoard it, we often find that it has gone. The unwritten law of life decrees that only shared happiness abides and grows. With our achievement comes a related responsibility to use our newly acquired understanding to serve our fellow man better, because through our victory over hardship, we are given a keener insight, and therefore a greater tolerance for similar problems of others.

So while we are enumerating our blessings, let us remember that among the greatest of these is the refining fire and the broadening experiences of enduring hardships.
April 26, 1958.

The following story was written by Zelma as she was en route to Los Angeles. At that time she had an injury to one of her toes which caused her to walk with a slight limp.

Memoirs on a Flight to Los Angeles

Mary Ann took me to the airport and we were assured that I could board the 935 flight to Atlanta. I was assigned seat A-1, first seat (window) in first class! How's that for prestige! The stewardess who checked my boarding pass told me when it was time to disembark, she'd help me! Wow! So I pretended to be ever so humbly grateful, but I didn't actually get down and lick her feet. I just tried to look as though I was willing to comply so I'd get electric cart service at Atlanta.

As soon as I was seated on the plane, a male steward came and said, "Mrs. Studebaker when we get to Atlanta, you just stay seated until the other passengers are off, then I will escort you into the terminal where the officer has a cart waiting to take you to Gate A-16 for flight 103 to LA." You'd have thought my hind end was made of pure gold! The plane landed on time. I came off with the pilot, copilot and navigator! And the officer said, "Mrs. Studebaker, here comes your electric cart. Can you get into it alone?" I said I thought I could make it! Then a little talkative black guy took me on a long journey from Gate A-33 to A-16. He said I had one hour and 16 minutes to wait. They assigned me to seat 3-F, again a window seat in First Class.

Sure glad I forgot to eat my baloney sandwich because they served an enormous four course luncheon of appetizers, large salad entrée, duck a' la orange, green beans, stuffed tomato, tiny browned potatoes, roll and dessert.

This is an easy comfortable flight at 35,000 feet. It is overcast beyond the Mississippi and pretty clear as we cross New Mexico into Arizona. The pilot says we will land on time in L.A. and it's 67 degrees now. This is a wide body bird, six seats across.

I'm here beside a solemn looking fiftyish businessman who doesn't talk. Just fiddles with his calculator and writes on legal paper. Looks like Dr. Hess only very puffy and ripe looking, like a muskmelon that hung on the vine too long! Very interesting.
October 27, 1986

Chapter 7

Brethren Retirement Community

"The most important thing that parents can teach their children
is how to get along without them."
Frank A. Clark

After having spent 10 winters in Florida, 1978 to 1988, Zelma and Stanley came to Ohio for Christmas. This time Zelma did not return to their Florida home after Christmas due to health concerns. She was cared for in the homes of her nearby children and their families for the next five years. Long periods of time were spent at the homes of Milton and Mary Ann Mishler in Troy, Oho and Ron and Evonne Studebaker in Ashville, Oho. But the majority of her time was spent with Linda Biller who lived in Indiana, Pennsylvania and then Columbus, Ohio. Months later she returned to Florida with Linda for a week as she wanted to clean and clear some unfinished business. A year later she returned to Florida with Doug to dispose of and sell some remaining items in preparation for selling their Florida home. While Zelma's health confined her to Ohio for medical care, Stanley's health was still good and he was able to return to Florida for three more winters from 1989 to 1992. During this period of time, he hoped that Zelma's health would improve so she would be able to join him in Florida, but her health did not improve. In December of 1992, Stanley sold the Florida property and returned to the Ohio farm.

Zelma stayed with her children for five years, from December of 1988 to September of 1993. She insisted on helping where she could and she did enjoy cooking, baking, making meals, working in the garden, doing laundry and many other jobs when she was able. She sometimes participated in other activities with the family by going to church, taking walks, shopping, eating out, playing the piano, playing Scrabble and visiting with her children and grandchildren. As Ron stated, "It was a privilege and blessing to have her with us. There were many good talks about life. It was a cross-generational learning experience that will be remembered by her children and grandchildren." It was a pleasure for Zelma to engage in family activities. Milton spent much time participating with her in crossword games. Large print was used to assist with her vision. With Milton's help at reading clues to her; she was able to engage in word games.

As Zelma stayed with her children she was kept busy with a large amount of mail that she received as well as phone calls and visitors. Sometimes the letters she received in the mail outnumbered those received by others in the house. She was an appreciated lady. Gradually, more complex health problems were developing. Linda, a registered nurse described them as follows: diabetes, renal insufficiency, hypertension, mitral valve regurgitation, retinopathy, cataracts, coronary artery disease, gastric ulcers and anemia. She was eventually put on insulin and learned home management from Linda who has expertise in the area of diabetes. As her vision gradually diminished, she continued to write letters and read large print books with the aid of a magnifying glass. She also listened to talking books, poetry and articles from magazines with the use of record and cassette players. When her vision continued to deteriorate making it difficult for her to read medication labels or measure her insulin injections, Linda asked her if she ever got depressed. "No," she said, "I haven't pushed that button yet." She continued pursuing activities with an optimistic attitude. As her walking became more difficult she gradually began to use a wheelchair for outings that were more strenuous.

She resisted going to the Brethren Retirement Community for convalescent care even with the many fragile health problems that she was experiencing each day. However, as time passed and life threatening problems were occurring almost on a daily basis, Zelma finally agreed that it was time for her to go to the Brethren Retirement Community in Greenville, Ohio. On September 20, 1993, she became a resident there in the medical care unit. Again she had many guests and phone calls and continued writing letters to friends and relatives. Even after she had completely lost her sight, she allowed loved ones to write letters for her. She even asked family members to buy Christmas gifts for her to give to her family.

Zelma recalled with fondness, her pastor of many years, Burton Wolf who was a loyal visitor during her days at the Brethren Retirement Community. He anointed her on two occasions. Mary Sue Rosenberger, a chaplain at the Brethren Retirement Community was also a frequent visitor. Zelma was delighted with her visits. Burton and Mary Sue were her friends for many years before she came to the retirement community. Blanche Dohner was another friend who lived near Zelma. They were church friends who knew one another for 20 years and had become true soulmates during the many times they shared at the Retirement Community.

Two months after Zelma began living at the Brethren Retirement Community, Stanley came to live there also. He became a resident on November 6, 1993 in the independent care area while Zelma lived in the intensive care unit. As he realized how fragile Zelma's health was and his own need for convalescent care, he was very gracious to Zelma and all the health care workers at the retirement facility. He valued the many friendships and the opportunity to talk to the caretakers and looked forward to his daily visits with Zelma.

In December of 1993, the family gathered in the Brick Room at the Brethren Retirement Community to celebrate what would be their last Christmas with Zelma. It was another delightful time of sharing with immediate and extended family and friends. The family realized how precious those moments were and how fortunate they were to have this Christmas time together. Zelma engaged in the sharing with the same happy appreciation as always.

She had the satisfaction of knowing that her family and loved ones were at a place in life that gave her peace. No matter what difficulties they had gone through or were encountering, she was at peace and proud of her family. It was fulfilling for her when she thought about her family, her 20 grandchildren and 25 great-grandchildren.

Throughout their 65 years of marriage, Zelma and Stanley shared many happy times; however they had many arguments and unhappy experiences in their relationship. One day when Nancy and Linda were at the retirement community, they arranged for Zelma and Stanley to directly exchange spoken words of forgiveness to one another, an experience that the entire family supported. They both willingly agreed to this conversation which happened in Zelma's room. When they exchanged words of forgiveness to one another, it was a moment of refreshment and relief for the entire family as well as Zelma and Stanley, to realize God's favor and the peace of mind that comes with forgiveness. As difficult as their relationship was, it has caused their children to search for ways to resolve problems and develop ways to strengthen their own relationships with those closest to them

During one of Ron's visits with Zelma at the retirement community, he related how she occasionally expressed her feelings to the Lord with strong emotion. On one occasion he heard her say, "There are only three singers in the choir, Lord. Now what do you want me to do?" Her expression in Ron's presence is a reminder of a scripture, "For while we are in this tent, we groan and are burdened, because we do not wish to be unclothed but to be clothed with our heavenly dwelling so that what is mortal may be swallowed up by life." 2 Corinthians 5:4. Zelma comfortably spoke of heaven during her conversations with Sue Rosenberg, the chaplain at the retirement community.

The guest register in her room contained written commentary from many relatives, friends and caretakers as they visited with Zelma. Upon reading the guest book commentary, the reader comes to realize that Zelma's life gave people cause to ponder important issues in life such as giving, supporting, connecting, friendship, listening, compassion, hope, etc. The following final messages were written by Zelma's caretakers on August 5, 1994:

> Just now we are saddened by the death of Zelma, but we are all at peace knowing that she is no longer suffering, but we know she is in a better place. We love her and will miss her dearly.
> All our prayers, the 3 to 11 shift

> Tonight when I arrived at work I learned that Zelma had finally achieved the desire of her heart – to be with her Lord. So often she would wonder why she would have to linger to be "Over the Sunset Mountains" and "Into the Arms of Jesus" who was truly the center of her life. I'm praying our Lord will always wrap his loving arms around Zelma's family and give them strength for the coming days.
> Barbara Stork, R.N.

> Zelma is a very special lady. I took care of her the very first day she came to the Brethren Retirement Community. Just knowing Zelma has really been special to me. Many times I read to her when she would want something read. I can always look forward to one of her hugs. Some people come into your heart and leave. Some people come into your life and leave footprints in your heart. And you are never the same. Zelma has left her footprints in my heart.
> Diane Butler, Nursing Assistant 3 to 11 shift.

Zelma was a woman of many talents. She had strong character, self-confidence, Christian values, a good sense of humor and an intuitive ability to accept and make changes as the times changed. She wasn't locked into a mold. She saw her own children participate in life and make contributions and she quietly reveled in it. She took pride in interacting with her family and supported their efforts with interest and rapport as they reached the various stages of their lives. She created a life where she could be around her family and friends, or at least in correspondence with them throughout her life. As a talented writer, Zelma delighted in expressing her thoughts in a way that held the attention of her audience. She truly enjoyed the sharing and the deep appreciation for the responses that were reciprocated back to her.

Zelma was a service oriented person and her style was that of inclusion. She had the unusual ability to accept the many differences that people presented. She engaged in these settings in a comfortable, poised manner. She was skillful at perceiving what people needed and was willing to take whatever time was necessary to seek a positive outcome about life's perplexities and do it in a non-threatening way.

If there was no light at the end of the tunnel, she tried to help you find it. Such a life style brought about hope and sometimes healing. She was familiar with struggle and confrontation but she also knew the wisdom of perseverance. Hers was a life that was disciplined by humanitarian values. She stated that she depended on the strength that God gave her. She enjoyed much fulfillment in her life but she also dealt with many difficult moments and even the tragedy of her son's death. Through it all she knew that God in his vigilance had a plan for her life and provided a measure of, as she said, "inner strength" as well as purpose in her journey.

Years after she went to her heavenly home, her humanitarian life continues to be pondered as well as celebrated. Her impact on family communication and tradition are continuing. With ambition and pride she participated with family and friends and even through the difficult times she could radiate hope because she had hope. She possessed the very qualities that are treasured by so many.

Chapter 8

Remembering a Heritage

"It is not the honor that you take with you, but the heritage you leave behind."
Branch Rickey

For those who knew her, Zelma imparted characteristics that they chose to embrace. Accordingly, her influence has been the stimulus for family traditions that her own children continue. These include the annual bed and breakfast reunions with the production of booklets and photos, the cousins' picnic, the family directory (birthdates, anniversaries and contact information), publications of family biographies, songs, and poems. Stanley also took pride in family heritage and influenced these same family traditions. Their children are aware that these various activities reflect the appreciation they have for their parents. Such a heritage is without a doubt a matter of pride. Some of the grandchildren have plans to continue these same family traditions with their own extended relatives.

The Bed and Breakfast Reunions

In 1996 the annual bed and breakfast reunions were started by the children of Zelma and Stanley Studebaker with spouses also participating. Each year the bed and breakfast reunions are held at a different location throughout the country with each child taking turns hosting the event.

Soon after the first few reunions, the siblings added a writing assignment about family memories and personal interests. Each family member reads his/her assignment at one of the evenings of the reunion. At the conclusion of each gathering, Gary, the family historian, composes a written report of the reunion which includes the assignments, photos and information about the location of the reunion and sends a copy of the booklet to each family member to share with their family and friends.

As a result of the bed and breakfast reunions, numerous benefits have been realized including the delight of seeing a different part of the country, the healthy anticipation of a vacation, family sharing and having a written account of each reunion to share with extended family and friends.

Bed and Breakfast Reunions of the Children of Zelma and Stanley Studebaker

Year	Location	Host	Assignment	Booklet Title
1996	Springfield, OH	Mary Ann Nancy	Visiting. Touring local sites	
1997	Sugar Creek, OH	Ron	Visiting. Touring local sites	
1998	Camden, OH	Lowell	Visiting. Touring local sites	
1999	Granville, OH	Linda	Visiting. Touring local sites	
2000	Calistoga, CA	Gary Doug	Write your autobiography	The Calistoga Seven
2001	London, OH	Mary Ann	Write about things you've learned growing up	Things I Learned Growing Up
2002	Urbana, OH	Nancy	Write questions for Mom and Dad	Questions for Mom and Dad
2003	Lebanon, OH	Ron	Write about family memories	Memories of Your Siblings
2004	Sevierville, TN	Lowell	Nieces and nephews write about their aunts and uncles	The Smoky Mountain Summit
2005	Port Townsend, WA	Linda	Exploring the Seattle area waterways	The Port Townsend Party
2006	Laguna Beach, CA	Gary	Siblings write about their children	The Laguna Beach Bash
2007	Cincinnati, OH	Mary Ann	Share about the published family cookbook	The Cincinnati Celebration
2008	Half Moon Bay, CA	Doug	Share something personal and positive. Trivia questions and answers	The Half Moon Bay Happening
2009	South Bend, IN	Nancy	Write about family food and meal memories	Siblings in South Bend
2010	Yellowstone National Park, WY	Linda	Write your personal health info and little known facts about yourself	The Yellowstone Story
2011	Kennebunkport, ME	Ron	Write 2 haikus, good things about aging and your bucket list	The Kennebunkport Connection
2012	Flagstaff, AZ	Lowell	Talk with visuals by Doug and Gary regarding their visit to Vietnam in May of 2012 to honor Ted.	Flagstaff Festivities
2013	Portland, OR	Gary	Write about what gives you hope. Phyllis Cribby visit.	The Portland Pow Wow

Year	Location	Host	Assignment	Booklet Title
2014	Vancouver, Canada	Doug	A filmed interview about Ted's life for the Dayton Peace Museum	Vancouver Vibes
2015	Richmond, IN	Mary Ann	Update your autobiography and your bucket list	The Richmond Reunion
2016	Charleston, SC	Nancy	Sing or read three songs that express your thoughts	Chillin' in Charleston
2017	Leavenworth, WA	Linda	Write about a difficulty you encountered, the results and lessons learned	Levity in Leavenworth

Five of the reunions included a celebration of the life of Ted Studebaker for his courageous contributions to peace:

	Reunion	Celebrating Ted's Life
2007	Cincinnati, OH	A visit to the Dayton International Peace Museum to see the peace displays.
2012	Flagstaff, AZ	Doug and Gary reported on their trip to Vietnam where they visited Ted's village, colleagues and locations where he worked.
2013	Portland, OR	A visit and talk with Phyllis Cribby, Ted's VNCS colleague.
2014	Vancouver, Canada	Ted's siblings were interviewed as they were filmed for Ted's exhibit at the Dayton International Peace Museum.
2015	Richmond, IN	A visit to the Dayton International Peace Museum and a review of Ted's exhibit.

The Cousins Picnic

The annual cousin's picnic started in 1954. It is a reunion for all extended family members from the Studebaker and Roth families. The picnic is usually held at or near the Troy, Ohio area. Alison Bucchi has planned and organized these reunions.

The Studebaker Directory

With the continually growing extended family, Milton and Mary Ann began producing an annual updated family directory of the children and extended family of Zelma and Stanley. The first Studebaker Directory was produced in 1981. As of this writing, the Directory continues to keep the family apprised of updated addresses, telephone numbers, birthdates and wedding anniversaries. Over the years, several family members have accepted the responsibility of gathering this information, producing the updated Directory and e-mailing it to each family. The Directory has been a useful resource for corresponding with one another and a convenient reminder of the important occasions in each person's life.

It is a fair evaluation to conclude that Zelma influenced the writing traditions of all of her children as observed from their narratives and poetry recorded from the annual bed and breakfast reunions and other publications. It was Zelma who took pride at encouraging her children as they wrote papers for their course work in the areas of humanitarian values and responsible citizenship. She also encouraged the use of diaries and writing journals. Sometimes she provided a diary or journal to a loved one for recording their daily accounts or stories as they were preparing to embark on journey or service assignment. Before Stanley flew to west coast, Zelma gave a writing journal to him and suggested a written account of his trip which he did. His journal was a significant part of his published biography.

Publications from the Family of Zelma and Stanley Studebaker

1) Studebaker, Gary W. and Amy Powell. The Queen of Hearts, The Life of Zelma Louise Roth Studebaker, 2nd edition. Eugene, OR: Wipf and Stock Publishers, 2018.

2) Mishler, Mary Ann. A Taste of Tradition, Fletcher, OH: Friends and Family Cookbook Publishers, 2007. The cookbook contains family recipes, photos, food related stories and traditions associated with meals, picnics and food preparation.

3) Studebaker, Gary W. Everything is Copacetic, The Life of Stanley Studebaker. Anaheim, CA: TheSpectrumPress@gmail.com, 2015.

4) Studebaker, Gary W. and Douglas E. Studebaker. Ted Allen Studebaker, An Enduring Force for Peace. Eugene, OR: Wipf and Stock Publishers, 2017.

5) Studebaker, Gary W. Choice Words. Baltimore, MD: Publish America, 2008.

6) Studebaker, Gary W. Piercing Truths. Baltimore, MD: Publish America, 2009.

7) Studebaker, Gary W. Autism Spectrum Realities, Charleston, SC: TheSpectrumPress@gmail.com, 2011

8) Studebaker, Gary W. "Ted Studebaker in Vietnam." Producer Steve Engle. [Music CD]. Alexandria, PA: Dunkertown Records, 2005.

9) Studebaker, Gary W. "Heroes and Friends." Producer Tim Kearns. [Music CD]. Fullerton, CA: S1 Studios: 2015.

Zelma was proud to acknowledge her Christian heritage. "Upon coming to America my ancestors were admonished to hold fast to their faith in God. They followed scriptural teachings for the glory of God and their neighbor's good." She explained that Bible reading was a regular habit in her home as she grew up. It was her father who led the family in scripture reading and prayer each evening. She stated that honesty and obedience were reinforced by Bible stories. By the same token, the back of a hairbrush was not spared for such behavior as deceit, cheating, foul language and gossip. Since the Depression left many people without work and food, she learned to come to the aid of those in need of food.

Zelma was a forgiving person as she openly cited God's word as her basis for forgiving the person who was responsible for her son's death. Before Gary departed for his volunteer assignment in Laos, Zelma gave him his first Bible with a comment about the power of God's word for whatever situation he faced. She also gave him a dairy to record his observations while he was away from home. Before Ron boarded his flight for his volunteer assignment in Morocco, it was Zelma who expressed theses parting words to him. "Listen to your heart and do what is right." It was Zelma who accompanied Ted forward to dedicate his life to Jesus at a revival held at Milton-Union High School in 1956. Following a Sunday school discussion it was Zelma who continued the dialog at home by stating, "Our purpose in life is to serve Jesus by everything we do." Barbara Stork, one of Zelma's caretakers at the Brethren Retirement Community had many discussions with Zelma. It was Barbara who reminded us with her entry in Zelma's guest register that Zelma longed to be "in the arms of Jesus who was truly the center of her life."

Zelma was known for many things. She may have been the bard of poetry. She may have been the sage of scrabble. She may have been the guru of written communication. She may have won accolades for her acrobatics down the main street of heaven, but she is probably best described as The Queen of Hearts.

Appendix

Appendix A

Genealogy

Recorded here are Zelma's, maternal grandparents, Coelestine and Elnora Leiber and their eleven children with their respective spouses. Zelma's mother, Elnora was the eleventh and last child in this family. With the exception of 3 deaths at infancy, most of the children grew up and lived in or near Englewood, Ohio

Zelma's Maternal Grandparents.

Name	Born	Died	Age
Coelestine Leiber	1832	1916	84
Elnora Sunkle	1830	1896	66

Zelma's Aunts and Uncles, the Leibers

#	Name	Born	Died	Age
1)	Died in infancy			
2)	Died in infancy			
3)	Died in infancy			
4)	Fred Leiber	unknown		
	Mary Penrod (spouse)	unknown		
5)	Mary Leiber (Molly)	1851	1903	52
	Joe Toprano (spouse)	unknown		
6)	Caroline Leiber (Collie)	1861	1891	30
	John Sink (spouse)	unknown		
7)	Charles Leiber (Charlie)	1864	1940	76
	Louisa Laukhoff	1865	1939	74
8)	Augustus Leiber	1866	1960	94
	Blanche Vore	1873	1938	65
9)	Ed Leiber	1868	1957	89
	Anna Applegate	1873	1951	78
10)	Celestine Leiber (Les)	1871	1957	86
	Elizabeth Poling	1888	1972	84
11)	Ida Elnora (Nora) Leiber	1874	1953	79
	Fred Roth	1877	1952	75

The last entry on the chart above are Zelma's parents. The children of Fred and Elnora Roth in birth order are: Orville Edison (died at birth), Zelma, Emerson, Pauline and Loyal.

119

MARCH ON WASHINGTON FOR JOBS AND FREEDOM

AUGUST 28, 1963

LINCOLN MEMORIAL PROGRAM

1. The National Anthem — Led by Marian Anderson.

2. Invocation — The Very Rev. Patrick O'Boyle, *Archbishop of Washington.*

3. Opening Remarks — A. Philip Randolph, *Director March on Washington for Jobs and Freedom.*

4. Remarks — Dr. Eugene Carson Blake, *Stated Clerk, United Presbyterian Church of the U.S.A.; Vice Chairman, Commission on Race Relations of the National Council of Churches of Christ in America.*

5. Tribute to Negro Women Fighters for Freedom
   - Daisy Bates
   - Diane Nash Bevel
   - Mrs. Medgar Evers
   - Mrs. Herbert Lee
   - Rosa Parks
   - Gloria Richardson
   — Mrs. Medgar Evers

6. Remarks — John Lewis, *National Chairman, Student Nonviolent Coordinating Committee.*

7. Remarks — Walter Reuther, *President, United Automobile, Aerospace and Agricultural Implement Wokers of America, AFL-CIO; Chairman, Industrial Union Department, AFL-CIO.*

8. Remarks — James Farmer, *National Director, Congress of Racial Equality.*

9. Selection — Eva Jessye Choir

10. Prayer — Rabbi Uri Miller, *President Synagogue Council of America.*

11. Remarks — Whitney M. Young, Jr., *Executive Director, National Urban League.*

12. Remarks — Mathew Ahmann, *Executive Director, National Catholic Conference for Interracial Justice.*

13. Remarks — Roy Wilkins, *Executive Secretary, National Association for the Advancement of Colored People.*

14. Selection — Miss Mahalia Jackson

15. Remarks — Rabbi Joachim Prinz, *President American Jewish Congress.*

16. Remarks — The Rev. Dr. Martin Luther King, Jr., *President, Southern Christian Leadership Conference.*

17. The Pledge — A Philip Randolph

18. Benediction — Dr. Benjamin E. Mays, *President, Morehouse College.*

"WE SHALL OVERCOME"

Statement by the heads of the ten organizations calling for discipline in connection with the Washington March of August 28, 1963:

"The Washington March of August 28th is more than just a demonstration.

"It was conceived as an outpouring of the deep feeling of millions of white and colored American citizens that the time has come for the government of the United States of America, and particularly for the Congress of that government, to grant and guarantee complete equality in citizenship to the Negro minority of our population.

"As such, the Washington March is a living petition—in the flesh—of the scores of thousands of citizens of both races who will be present from all parts of our country.

"It will be orderly, but not subservient. It will be proud, but not arrogant. It will be non-violent, but not timid. It will be unified in purposes and behavior, not splintered into groups and individual competitors. It will be outspoken, but not raucous.

"It will have the dignity befitting a demonstration in behalf of the human rights of twenty millions of people, with the eye and the judgment of the world focused upon Washington, D.C., on August 28, 1963.

"In a neighborhood dispute there may be stunts, rough words and even hot insults; but when a whole people speaks to its government, the dialogue and the action must be on a level reflecting the worth of that people and the responsibility of that government.

"We, the undersigned, who see the Washington March as wrapping up the dreams, hopes, ambitions, tears, and prayers of millions who have lived for this day, call upon the members, followers and wellwishers of our several organizations to make the March a disciplined and purposeful demonstration.

"We call upon them all, black and white, to resist provocations to disorder and to violence.

"We ask them to remember that evil persons are determined to smear this March and to discredit the cause of equality by deliberate efforts to stir disorder.

"We call for self-discipline, so that no one in our own ranks, however enthusiastic, shall be the spark for disorder.

"We call for resistance to the efforts of those who, while not enemies of the March as such, might seek to use it to advance causes not dedicated primarily to civil rights or to the welfare of our country.

"We ask each and every one in attendance in Washington or in spiritual attendance back home to place the Cause above all else.

"Do not permit a few irresponsible people to hang a new problem around our necks as we return home. Let's do what we came to do—place the national human rights problem squarely on the doorstep of the national Congress and of the Federal Government.

"Let's win at Washington."

SIGNED:

Mathew Ahmann, *Executive Director of the National Catholic Conference for Interracial Justice.*

Reverend Eugene Carson Blake, *Vice-Chairman of the Commission on Race Relations of the National Council of Churches of Christ in America*

James Farmer, *National Director of the Congress of Racial Equality.*

Reverend Martin Luther King, Jr., *President of the Southern Christian Leadership Conference.*

John Lewis, *Chairman of the Student Nonviolent Coordinating Committee.*

Rabbi Joachim Prinz, *President of the American Jewish Congress.*

A. Philip Randolph, *President of the Negro American Labor Council.*

Walter Reuther, *President of the United Automobile, Aerospace and Agricultural Implement Workers of America, AFL-CIO, and Chairman,*

Industrial Union Department, AFL-CIO.

Roy Wilkins, *Executive Secretary of the National Association for the Advancement of Colored People.*

Whitney M. Young, Jr., *Executive Director of the National Urban League.*

In addition, the March has been endorsed by major religious, fraternal, labor and civil rights organizations. A full list, too long to include here, will be published.

WHAT WE DEMAND*

1. Comprehensive and effective civil rights legislation from the present Congress—without compromise or filibuster—to guarantee all Americans

    access to all public accommodations

    decent housing

    adequate and integrated education

    the right to vote

2. Withholding of Federal funds from all programs in which discrimination exists.

3. Desegregation of all school districts in 1963.

4. Enforcement of the Fourteenth Amendment—reducing Congressional representation of states where citizens are disfranchised.

5. A new Executive Order banning discrimination in all housing supported by federal funds.

6. Authority for the Attorney General to institute injunctive suits when any constitutional right is violated.

7. A massive federal program to train and place all unemployed workers—Negro and white—on meaningful and dignified jobs at decent wages.

8. A national minimum wage act that will give all Americans a decent standard of living. (Government surveys show that anything less than $2.00 an hour fails to do this.)

9. A broadened Fair Labor Standards Act to include all areas of employment which are presently excluded.

10. A federal Fair Employment Practices Act barring discrimination by federal, state, and municipal governments, and by employers, contractors, employment agencies, and trade unions.

*Support of the March does not necessarily indicate endorsement of every demand listed. Some organizations have not had an opportunity to take an official position on all of the demands advocated here.

121

Appendix C

Miami University

122

Studebaker honored for dedication

HANDSHAKE OF GRATITUDE — Mrs. Zelda Studebaker, retiring Valley Forge teacher, receives gratitude from PTO president Ed Underwood. Mrs. Studebaker has taught in Wayne for ten of her 19 teaching years.

years later she married and temporarily stopped teaching.

When her eighth child was in the third grade, in 1961, she returned to teaching.

In 1968, she graduated from Miami University.

She says she enjoys children and "exploring their world". Her own children have been involved in a social type of work such as teaching, nursing counseling.

One hobby Mrs. Studebaker is anxious to spend more time with is writing. She recently was asked to participate in the Mollie Hunter writing workshop at Wright State University.

Appendix E

ON A SATURDAY NIGHT
JOSEPH E. HOWARD
Chorus, Tempo di Valse
On A Sat - ur-day Night, Dear old Sat - ur-day night,
When your pock-ets are filled with coin; Ev - ry - bod - y is
asked to join; On A Sat - ur-day Night; Good old
Sat - ur-day Night. The next day is Sun - day, but still on a
Mon-day, We dream of Sat - ur-day night. night.

Appendix F

THE QUEEN OF HEARTS

Gary Studebaker
Copyright 1996

Not in - to dia - monds or pearls;
Beau - ti - ful poems we quote,

friend - ship, that was her world.
de - tailed let - ters she wrote; but I

Not in - to head - lines, not in - to dead - lines;
find I'm still liv - in' the val - ues she's giv - en, and

17   E   Eaug7   E7   A7

be all that you can be.   En- the
no mat - ter how far I roam   the

21   G   A   D   Bmin   D

cour - age - ment giv - er was she,   en -
mem' - ries still bring me back home,   yes the

25   G   A   D

cour - age - ment gi - ver was she.   She said
mem' - ries still bring me back home.

29   G   A   D   G

live what is faith - ful and true,   let the Lord guide the

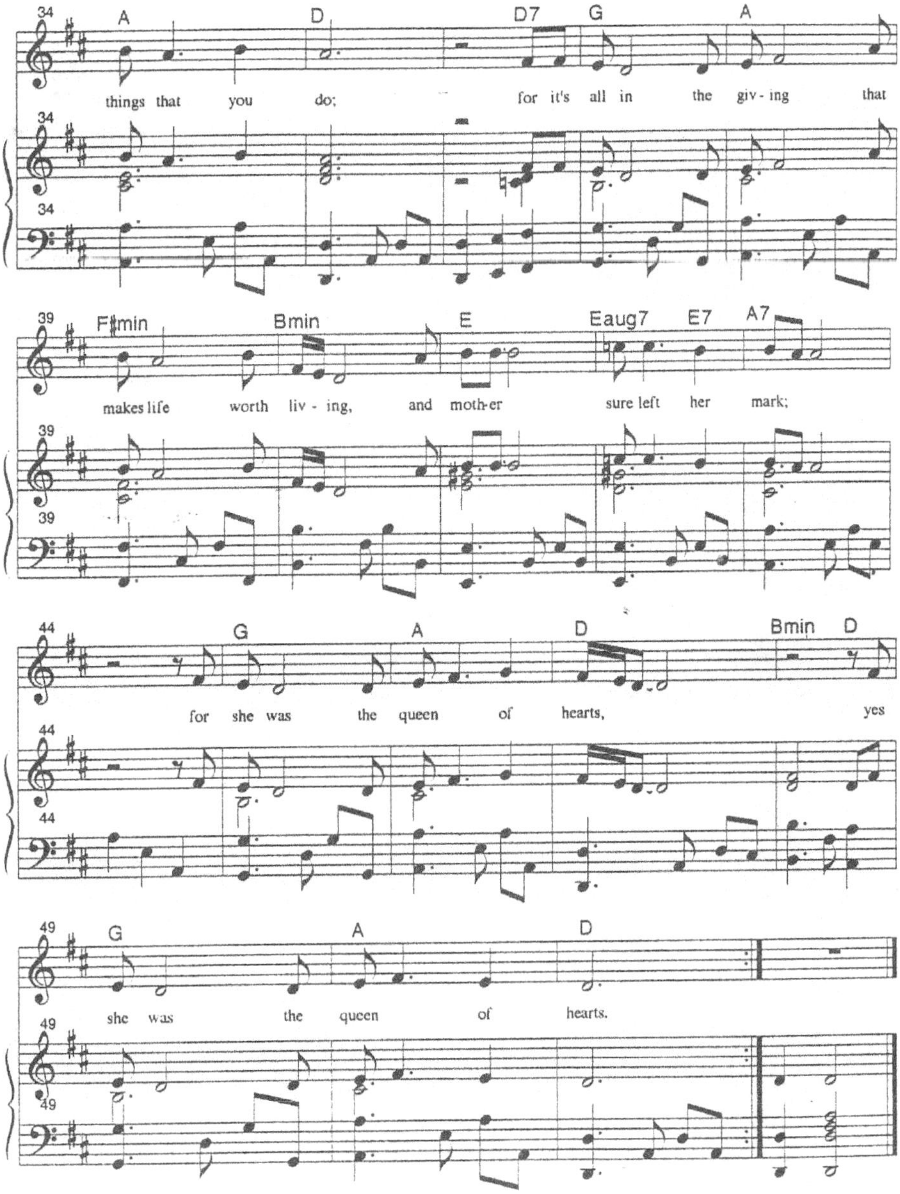
A D D7 G A
things that you do; for it's all in the giv - ing that
F♯min Bmin E Eaug7 E7 A7
makes life worth liv - ing, and moth-er sure left her mark;
G A D Bmin D
for she was the queen of hearts, yes
G A D
she was the queen of hearts.

About the Authors

Gary W. Studebaker is a son of Zelma and Stanley Studebaker. He was a volunteer agriculturalist in Laos and a special education teacher. He is a writer of family biographies and other publications. Gary and his wife Susan are the parents of a daughter.

Amy L. Powell is a granddaughter of Zelma and Stanley Studebaker. She had a career in business and was an elementary school teacher. Amy and her husband John are the parents of three children.

www.ingramcontent.com/pod-product-compliance
Lightning Source LLC
Chambersburg PA
CBHW080558090426
42735CB00016B/3276